3
ingredients...

3 ingredients Table of Contents

3 Fuss-Free Starters

ingredients

Rich & Meaty Pizza Cup Snacks

Prep Time: 10 minutes • **Cook Time:** 20 minutes

1 can (12 ounces)
 refrigerated biscuits
 (10 biscuits)
1½ cups RAGÚ® Rich &
 Meaty Meat Sauce
½ cup shredded mozzarella
 cheese (about
 2 ounces)

1. Preheat oven to 375°F. In 12-cup muffin pan, evenly press each biscuit in bottom and up side of each cup; chill until ready to fill.

2. Evenly spoon Meat Sauce into prepared muffin cups. Bake 15 minutes. Evenly sprinkle tops with cheese and bake an additional 5 minutes or until cheese is melted and biscuits are golden. Let stand 5 minutes before serving. Gently remove pizza cups from muffin pan and serve. *Makes 10 pizza cups*

Fast Pesto Focaccia

Prep and Cook Time: 20 minutes

1 can (10 ounces)
   refrigerated pizza crust
   dough
2 tablespoons prepared
   pesto
4 sun-dried tomatoes
   (packed in oil), drained

1. Preheat oven to 425°F. Lightly grease 8-inch square baking pan. Unroll pizza dough. Fold in half; press gently into pan.

2. Spread pesto evenly over dough. Chop tomatoes or snip with kitchen scissors; sprinkle over pesto. Press tomatoes into dough. Using wooden spoon handle, make indentations in dough every 2 inches.

3. Bake 10 to 12 minutes or until golden brown. Cut into 16 squares. Serve warm or at room temperature.

Makes 16 servings

Pepper and Parsley Logs

8 ounces cream cheese,
   softened
1 packet (1 ounce)
   HIDDEN VALLEY® The
   Original Ranch® Salad
   Dressing & Seasoning
   Mix
2 teaspoons cracked black
   pepper
2 teaspoons chopped fresh
   parsley

Combine cream cheese and salad dressing & seasoning mix in a medium bowl. Divide in half; chill until firm. Roll into two 1½-inch logs, coating one with pepper and the other with parsley. Wrap in plastic wrap; chill. *Makes 2 logs*

Serving Suggestion: Spread on crackers or bread.

FAST PESTO FOCACCIA

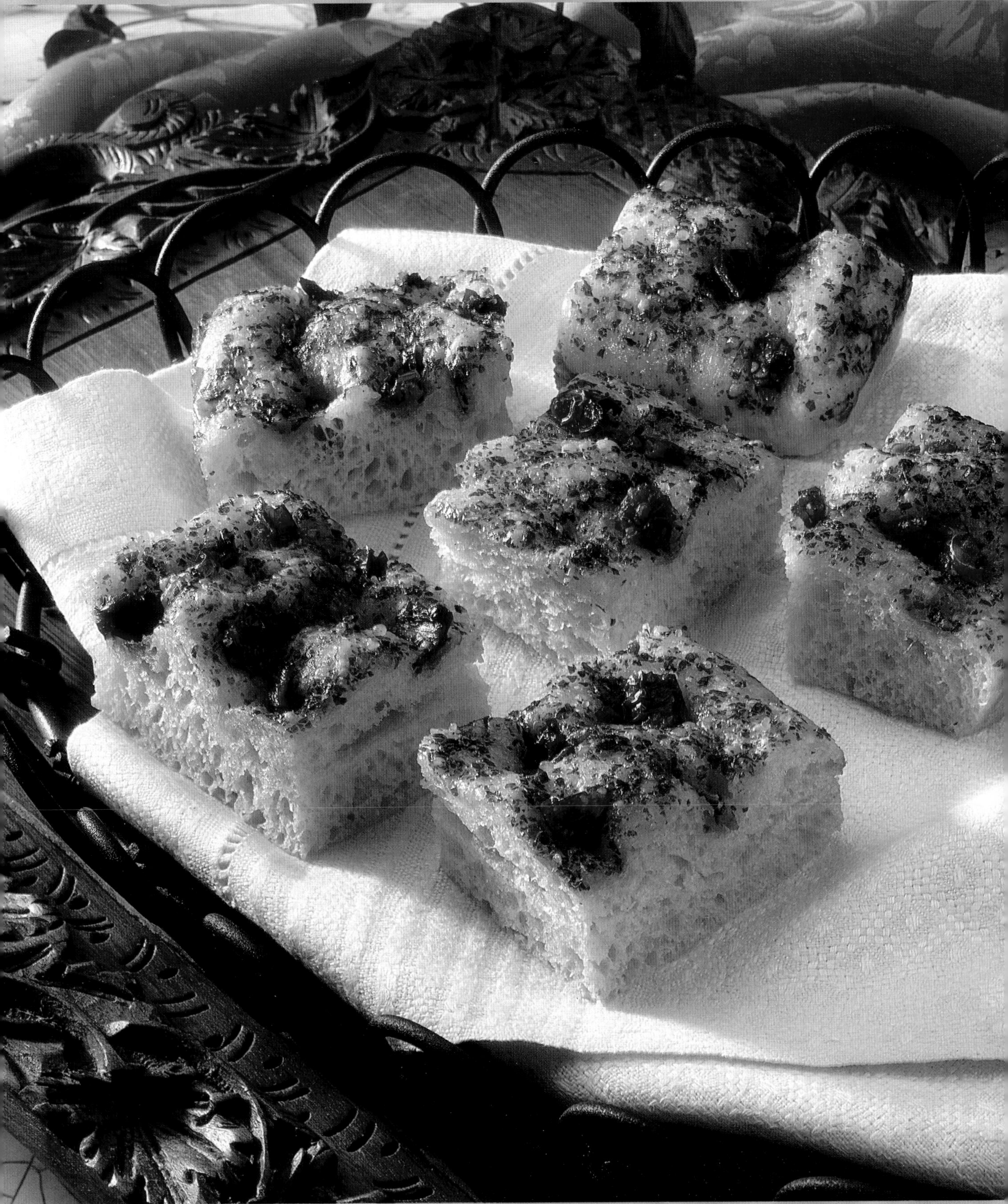

Crispy Tortilla Chicken

1½ cups crushed tortilla
    chips
1 package (1¼ ounces) taco
    seasoning mix
24 chicken drummettes
    Salsa (optional)

1. Preheat oven to 350°F. Spray large rimmed baking sheet with nonstick cooking spray.

2. Combine tortilla chips and taco seasoning in large shallow bowl. Coat chicken with crumb mixture, turning to coat all sides. Shake off excess crumbs; place chicken on prepared baking sheet.

3. Bake 40 minutes or until chicken is no longer pink in center. Serve with salsa, if desired. *Makes 24 appetizers*

Baked Vidalia Onion Dip

Prep Time: 10 minutes • **Cook Time:** 25 minutes

1 cup chopped Vidalia
    onion
1 cup grated Parmesan
    cheese or shredded
    Swiss cheese (about
    4 ounces)
1 cup HELLMANN'S® or
    BEST FOODS® Real
    Mayonnaise
1 clove garlic, finely
    chopped (optional)
    Hot pepper sauce to taste
    (optional)

1. Preheat oven to 375°F.

2. In 1-quart casserole, combine all ingredients. Bake uncovered 25 minutes or until golden brown. Serve with your favorite dippers. *Makes 2 cups dip*

CRISPY TORTILLA CHICKEN

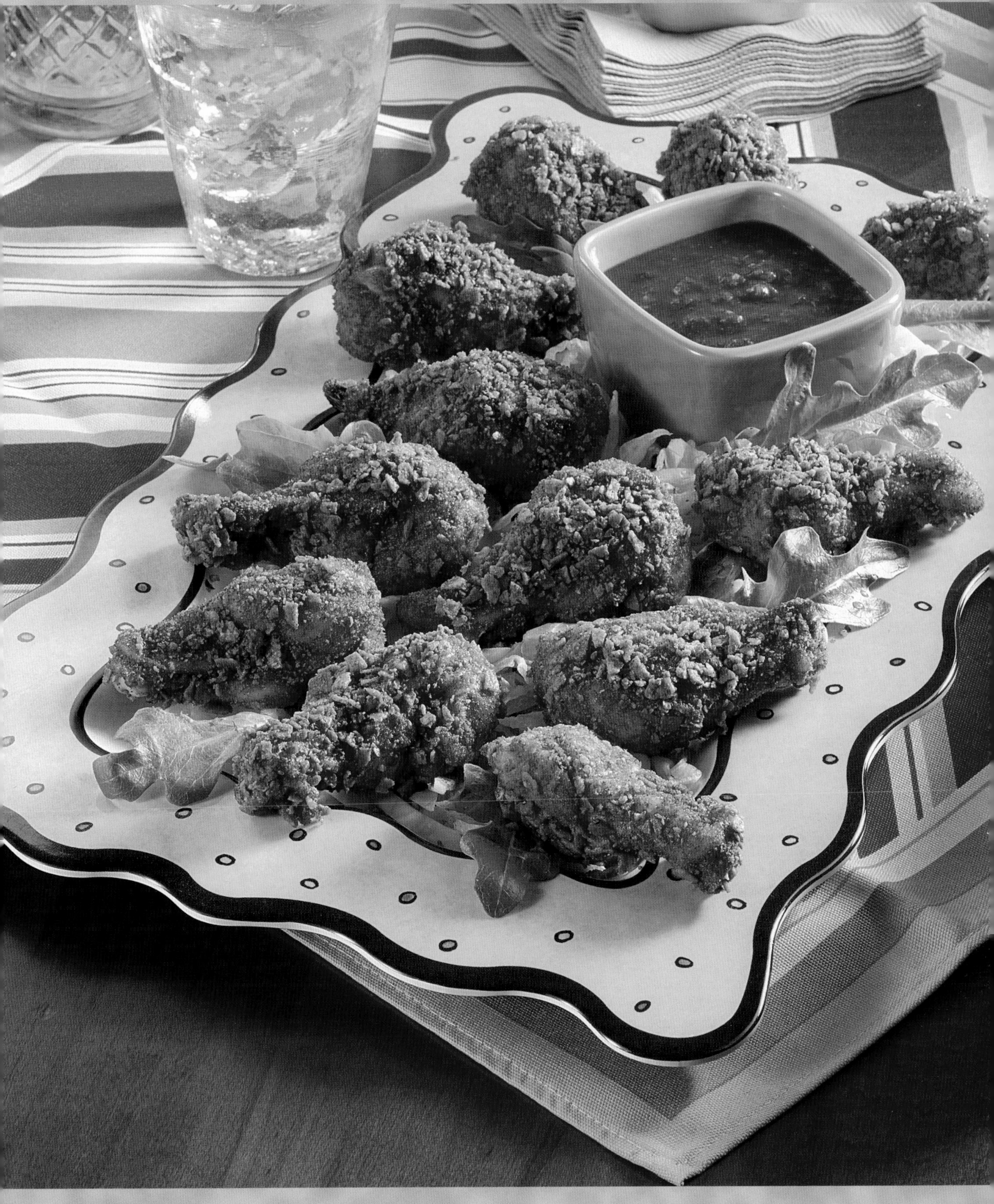

3
ingredients

Bacon-Wrapped Breadsticks

8 slices bacon
16 garlic-flavored
    breadsticks (about
    8 inches long)
¾ cup grated Parmesan
    cheese
2 tablespoons chopped
    fresh parsley (optional)

1. Cut bacon slices in half lengthwise. Wrap half slice of bacon diagonally around each breadstick. Combine Parmesan cheese and parsley, if desired, in shallow dish; set aside.

2. Place 4 breadsticks on double layer of paper towels in microwave oven. Microwave on HIGH 2 to 3 minutes or until bacon is cooked through. Immediately roll breadsticks in Parmesan mixture to coat. Repeat with remaining breadsticks.

Makes 16 breadsticks

Cracker Bites

Prep Time: 15 minutes

1 pound JENNIE-O TURKEY
    STORE® Deli Premium
    Seasoned Brown Sugar
    Roasted Turkey Breast,
    thinly shaved
1 (4.25-ounce) package
    CARR'S® Water
    Crackers, 3-inch size
¾ cup (6 ounces) pineapple
    preserves

Mound about ½ ounce of JENNIE-O TURKEY STORE® Premium Seasoned Brown Sugar Turkey Breast on each cracker. Dollop with about 1 teaspoon of preserves.

Place on serving platter; garnish with fresh pineapple spears, if desired.

Makes about 3 dozen appetizers

Variations: Any variety of JENNIE-O TURKEY STORE® turkey breast can be used in this recipe. Any thick preserve could be used instead of pineapple. Substitute dark cherry, apricot or peach preserves.

3
ingredients

Holiday Appetizer Puffs

1 sheet frozen puff pastry,
   thawed (half of
   17¼-ounce package)
2 tablespoons olive or
   vegetable oil
   Toppings: grated
   Parmesan cheese,
   sesame seeds, poppy
   seeds or dried basil

1. Preheat oven to 425°F. Roll out pastry on lightly floured surface into 13-inch square. Cut out shapes with cookie cutters. (Simple shapes work best.) Place on ungreased baking sheets.

2. Brush cutouts lightly with oil; sprinkle with desired topping.

3. Bake 6 to 8 minutes or until golden. Serve warm or at room temperature.

Makes about 1½ dozen appetizers

Watermelon Kebobs

18 cubes (1-inch) seedless
   watermelon
 6 ounces (1-inch cubes)
   fat-free turkey breast
 6 ounces (1-inch cubes)
   reduced-fat Cheddar
   cheese
 6 drinking straws or 6-inch
   bamboo skewers

Alternate cubes of watermelon between cubes of turkey and cheese threaded onto each straw, as shown in photo.

Makes 6 servings

Favorite recipe from *National Watermelon Promotion Board*

helpful hint:

A ripe watermelon will have a shrunken, discolored stem and will produce a hollow sound when thumped with your knuckles. When choosing cut watermelon, look for bright-colored flesh with black seeds. The end nearest the stem is usually the sweetest. Avoid cut melon with coarse pale flesh, dark wet-looking flesh (overripe) or an abundance of small white seeds (underripe).

3
ingredients

Golden Chicken Nuggets

Prep Time: 5 minutes • **Cook Time:** 15 minutes

1 pound boneless skinless chicken, cut into 1½-inch pieces

¼ cup *French's®* Honey Mustard

2 cups *French's®* French Fried Onions, finely crushed

1. Preheat oven to 400°F. Toss chicken with mustard in medium bowl.

2. Place French Fried Onions into resealable plastic food storage bag. Toss chicken in onions, a few pieces at a time, pressing gently to adhere.

3. Place nuggets in shallow baking pan. Bake 15 minutes or until chicken is no longer pink in center. Serve with additional honey mustard. *Makes 4 servings*

Chutney Cheese Dip

1 (8-ounce) package cream cheese, softened

1 (8-ounce) container plain yogurt

½ cup chopped PATAK'S® Major Grey Mango Chutney

In medium bowl, combine all ingredients. Cover and refrigerate until serving time. Serve with fruit and crackers.

Makes 2½ cups dip

3

ingredients

Creamy Garlic Salsa Dip

1 envelope LIPTON®
 RECIPE SECRETS®
 Savory Herb with
 Garlic Soup Mix*
1 container (16 ounces)
 sour cream
½ cup your favorite
 prepared salsa

*Also terrific with LIPTON®
RECIPE SECRETS® Onion
Soup Mix.*

1. In medium bowl, combine all ingredients; chill if desired.

2. Serve with your favorite dippers.

Makes 2½ cups dip

Vegetable Cream Cheese

Prep Time: 10 minutes • **Chill Time:** 2 hours

1 envelope LIPTON®
 RECIPE SECRETS®
 Vegetable Soup Mix
2 packages (8 ounces each)
 cream cheese, softened
2 tablespoons milk

1. In medium bowl, combine all ingredients; chill 2 hours.

2. Serve on bagels or with assorted fresh vegetables.

Makes 2½ cups spread

Pinwheel Ham Bites

Prep Time: 30 minutes • **Chill Time:** 2 hours

2 packages (6½ ounces
   each) garlic-and-herb
   spreadable cheese
4 (¹⁄₁₆-inch-thick) slices
   boiled ham
40 rich round crackers

1. Spread ½ package cheese to edges of each ham slice. Beginning at short end, roll up tightly. Wrap tightly in plastic wrap; refrigerate rolls at least 2 hours.

2. Cut each roll crosswise into 10 slices. Place 1 slice on each cracker. Serve immediately.   *Makes 40 appetizers*

Sticky Wings

24 chicken wings (about
   4 pounds)
¾ cup WISH-BONE® Italian
   Dressing*
1 cup apricot or peach
   preserves
1 tablespoon hot pepper
   sauce (optional)**

Also terrific with WISH-BONE® Robusto Italian or Just 2 Good! Dressing.

**Use more or less to taste as desired.*

Cut tips off chicken wings (save tips for soup). Cut chicken wings in half at joint.

For marinade, blend Italian dressing, preserves and hot pepper sauce. In large, shallow nonaluminum baking dish or plastic bag, pour ½ of the marinade over chicken wings; toss to coat. Cover, or close bag, and marinate in refrigerator, turning occasionally, 3 to 24 hours. Refrigerate remaining marinade.

Remove wings, discarding marinade. Grill or broil wings, turning once and brushing frequently with refrigerated marinade, until wings are thoroughly cooked.   *Makes 48 appetizers*

3
ingredients

Lipton® Roasted Red Pepper & Onion Dip

1 envelope LIPTON®
 RECIPE SECRETS®
 Onion Soup Mix*
1 container (16 ounces)
 regular or light sour
 cream
1 jar (7 ounces) roasted red
 peppers, drained and
 chopped

*Also terrific with LIPTON®
RECIPE SECRETS® Savory
Herb with Garlic Soup Mix.

1. In small bowl, combine all ingredients; chill at least 2 hours.

2. Serve with your favorite dippers.

Makes 2 cups dip

Baked Brie

Prep Time: 3 minutes • **Cook Time:** 10 minutes

½ pound Brie cheese, rind
 removed
¼ cup chopped pecans
¼ cup KARO® Dark Corn
 Syrup

1. Preheat oven to 350°F. Place cheese in shallow oven-safe serving dish. Top with pecans and corn syrup.

2. Bake 8 to 10 minutes or until cheese is almost melted.

3. Serve warm with plain crackers or melba toast.

Makes 8 servings

3 ingredients

Buffalo Chicken Wing Sampler

Prep Time: 5 minutes • **Cook Time:** 12 minutes

2½ **pounds chicken wing pieces**
½ **cup** *Frank's® RedHot® Original Cayenne Pepper Sauce*
⅓ **cup melted butter**

1. Deep-fry* wings in hot oil (400°F) for 12 minutes until fully cooked and crispy; drain.

2. Combine **Frank's RedHot** Sauce and butter. Dip wings in sauce to coat.

3. Serve wings with celery and blue cheese dressing, if desired.

Makes 8 appetizer servings

For equally crispy wings, bake 1 hour at 425°F, or grill 30 minutes over medium heat.

RedHot® Sampler Variations: Add one of the following to **RedHot** butter mixture; heat through. Tex-Mex: 1 tablespoon chili powder, ¼ teaspoon garlic powder. Asian: 2 tablespoons honey, 2 tablespoons teriyaki sauce, 2 teaspoons ground ginger. Sprinkle wings with 1 tablespoon sesame seeds. Zesty Honey-Dijon: Substitute the following blend instead of the **RedHot** butter mixture—¼ cup each **Frank's® RedHot®** Sauce, **French's®** Honey Dijon Mustard and honey.

3 Satisfying Sides

ingredients

1 package (11 ounces) refrigerated French bread dough
1 tablespoon olive oil
½ teaspoon dried basil (optional)
1 tablespoon grated Parmesan cheese

Pullaparts

Prep Time: 5 minutes • **Bake Time:** 22 to 24 minutes

1. Preheat oven to 350°F.

2. Place dough on cutting board. Gently cut dough with serrated knife into 12 pieces.

3. Coat 9-inch round baking pan with butter-flavored cooking spray. Brush dough pieces lightly with oil. Arrange dough pieces almost touching each other in pan. Sprinkle with basil, if desired. Bake 22 to 24 minutes or until golden and rolls sound hollow when gently tapped. Remove from oven to wire rack.

4. Lightly spray tops of rolls with cooking spray. Sprinkle with cheese.

Makes 12 servings

Steamed Broccoli & Carrots

1 pound broccoli
12 baby carrots*
1 tablespoon butter

Substitute ½ pound frozen baby carrots or ½ pound regular carrots, cut into 2-inch chunks, for baby carrots.

1. Break broccoli into florets. Trim and discard large stems. Trim smaller stems; cut stems into thin slices.

2. Place 2 to 3 inches of water and steamer basket in large saucepan; bring water to a boil.

3. Add broccoli and carrots; cover. Steam 6 minutes or until vegetables are crisp-tender.

4. Place vegetables in serving bowl. Add butter; toss lightly to coat. Season to taste with salt and black pepper.

Makes 4 servings

Original Ranch® & Cheddar Bread

2 cups (8 ounces) shredded sharp Cheddar cheese
1 cup HIDDEN VALLEY® The Original Ranch® Salad Dressing
1 whole loaf (1 pound) French bread (not sourdough)

Combine cheese and salad dressing in a medium bowl. Cut bread in half lengthwise. Place on a broiler pan and spread dressing mixture evenly over cut side of each half. Broil until lightly brown. Cut each half into 8 pieces.

Makes 16 pieces

3 ingredients

Cob Corn in Barbecue Butter

4 ears fresh corn, shucked
2 tablespoons butter,
   softened
½ teaspoon dry barbecue
   seasoning

1. Pour 1 inch of water into large saucepan or skillet. (Do not add salt as it will make corn tough.) Bring to a boil over medium-high heat. Add corn; cover. Cook 4 to 6 minutes* or until kernels are slightly crisp when pierced with fork.

2. Remove corn with tongs to warm serving platter. Combine butter, barbecue seasoning and ¼ teaspoon salt in small bowl; stir until smooth. Serve immediately with corn.   *Makes 4 servings*

Length of cooking time depends on size and age of corn.

Oven-Roasted Vegetables

1 envelope LIPTON®
   RECIPE SECRETS®
   Savory Herb with
   Garlic Soup Mix*
1½ pounds assorted fresh
   vegetables**
2 tablespoons BERTOLLI®
   Olive Oil

*Also terrific with LIPTON®
RECIPE SECRETS® Onion or
Golden Onion Soup Mix.*

**Use any combination of the
following, sliced: zucchini;
yellow squash; red, green or
yellow bell peppers; carrots;
celery or mushrooms.*

1. Preheat oven to 450°F. In large plastic bag or bowl, combine all ingredients. Close bag and shake, or toss in bowl, until vegetables are evenly coated.

2. In 13×9-inch baking or roasting pan, arrange vegetables; discard bag.

3. Bake uncovered, stirring once, 20 minutes or until vegetables are tender.   *Makes 4 servings*

3
ingredients

Slow Cooker Cheddar Polenta

7 cups hot water

2 cups polenta (not "quick-cooking") or coarse-ground yellow cornmeal

2 tablespoons extra-virgin olive oil

2 teaspoons salt

3 cups grated CABOT® Extra Sharp or Sharp Cheddar (about 12 ounces)

SLOW COOKER DIRECTIONS

1. Combine water, polenta, olive oil and salt in slow cooker; whisk until well blended. Add cheese and whisk again.

2. Cover and cook on HIGH setting for 2 hours or until most liquid is absorbed. Stir well. (Polenta should have consistency of thick cooked cereal.) *Makes 8 servings*

Note: If not serving polenta right away, pour onto oiled baking sheet with sides, spreading into even layer; cover with plastic wrap and let cool. When ready to serve, cut polenta into rectangles and sauté in nonstick skillet with olive oil until golden on both sides.

Savory Skillet Broccoli

Prep Time: 5 minutes • **Cook Time:** 10 minutes

1 tablespoon BERTOLLI® Olive Oil

6 cups fresh broccoli florets *or* 1 pound green beans, trimmed

1 envelope LIPTON® RECIPE SECRETS® Golden Onion Soup Mix*

1½ cups water

*Also terrific with LIPTON® RECIPE SECRETS® Onion Mushroom Soup Mix.

1. In 12-inch skillet, heat oil over medium-high heat and cook broccoli, stirring occasionally, 2 minutes.

2. Stir in soup mix blended with water. Bring to a boil over high heat.

3. Reduce heat to medium-low and simmer covered 6 minutes or until broccoli is tender. *Makes 4 servings*

Cauliflower with Onion Butter

½ cup (1 stick) butter, divided
1 cup diced onion
1 large head cauliflower, cut into 2½×2-inch florets

1. Melt ¼ cup (½ stick) butter in medium skillet over medium heat. Add onion; cook and stir until onion is brown, about 20 minutes.

2. Meanwhile, place cauliflower and ½ cup water in microwavable bowl. Microwave on HIGH 8 minutes or until crisp-tender; drain if necessary.

3. Add remaining butter to skillet with onion; cook and stir until butter is melted. Pour over cooked cauliflower; serve immediately.

Scalloped Garlic Potatoes

3 medium all-purpose potatoes, peeled and thinly sliced (about 1½ pounds)
1 envelope LIPTON® RECIPE SECRETS® Savory Herb with Garlic Soup Mix
1 cup (½ pint) whipping or heavy cream
½ cup water

1. Preheat oven to 375°F. In lightly greased 2-quart shallow baking dish, arrange potatoes. In medium bowl, blend remaining ingredients; pour over potatoes.

2. Bake, uncovered, 45 minutes or until potatoes are tender.

Makes 4 servings

helpful hint:

There are many varieties of potatoes, so select them based on their intended use. Long whites are an all-purpose potato with thin pale brown skin. They average about eight ounces each. They can be baked, boiled or fried.

3
ingredients

Saucy Vegetable Casserole

Prep Time: 5 minutes • **Cook Time:** 20 minutes

2 bags (16 ounces each)
   frozen mixed
   vegetables (broccoli,
   cauliflower, carrots),
   thawed
2 cups *French's®* French
   Fried Onions, divided
1 package (16 ounces)
   pasteurized process
   cheese, cut into ¼-inch
   slices

1. Preheat oven to 350°F. Combine vegetables and *1 cup* French Fried Onions in shallow 3-quart baking dish. Top evenly with cheese slices.

2. Bake 15 minutes or until hot and cheese is almost melted; stir. Top with remaining *1 cup* onions and bake 5 minutes or until onions are golden.

Makes 8 servings

Variation: For added Cheddar flavor, substitute *French's® Cheddar French Fried Onions* for the original flavor.

Rice Pilaf Greek Style

2 cups chicken broth, beef
   broth or water
1 cup uncooked long-grain
   rice
1 tablespoon FILIPPO
   BERIO® Olive Oil
   Grated Parmesan or
   Romano cheese
   (optional)
   Toasted pine nuts
   (optional)

In 3-quart saucepan, combine chicken broth, rice and olive oil. Bring to a boil over medium-high heat; stir once. Cover; reduce heat to low and simmer 15 minutes or until rice is tender and liquid is absorbed. Remove from heat; let stand, covered, 5 to 10 minutes. Season to taste with salt and black pepper. Serve plain, or topped with cheese or pine nuts, if desired.

Makes 4 to 6 servings

3
ingredients

Rich & Creamy Mashed Cauliflower

Prep Time: 5 minutes • **Cook Time:** 15 minutes

1½ quarts water
1 medium head cauliflower, separated into florets (about 5 cups)
1 clove garlic, peeled
¼ cup HELLMANN'S® or BEST FOODS® Real or Light Mayonnaise or Just 2 Good!™ Reduced Fat Mayonnaise Dressing
¼ teaspoon salt
1 tablespoon chopped fresh basil leaves (optional)

1. In 3-quart saucepot, bring water to a boil. Add cauliflower and garlic. Cook covered 15 minutes or until florets are tender; drain.

2. In food processor or blender, process cauliflower, garlic, Hellmann's or Best Foods Real Mayonnaise and salt until creamy, scraping down sides as needed. Stir in basil and serve immediately.
Makes 5 servings

Pesto Double-Stuffed Potatoes

Prep and Cook Time: 45 minutes

4 large Idaho Potatoes, baked
½ cup part-skim ricotta cheese
⅓ cup prepared pesto
¼ teaspoon salt
¼ teaspoon black pepper

1. Preheat oven to 450°F.

2. Cut ½ inch from long side of each potato into bowl; scoop out inside of potato, leaving ¼-inch-thick shell. With fork or potato masher, mash cooked potato in bowl. Stir in ricotta, pesto, salt and pepper until well blended. Spoon potato mixture into potato shells, dividing evenly, heaping on top if necessary.

3. Lightly spray cookie sheet with nonstick cooking spray; place stuffed potatoes on cookie sheet. Bake until golden brown and heated through, about 10 to 15 minutes.
Makes 4 servings

Favorite recipe from **Idaho Potato Commission**

Broccoli with Cheese Sauce

MICROWAVE DIRECTIONS

1. Arrange broccoli florets on microwavable dinner plate with stems toward outside of plate; cover with vented plastic wrap. Microwave on HIGH 3 to 4 minutes or until broccoli stems are tender.

2. Combine cheese, milk and Worcestershire sauce, if desired, in 2-quart glass measuring cup. Microwave on HIGH 2 minutes; stir. If cheese is not completely melted, microwave 1 minute more, stirring after 30 seconds, until melted. Serve sauce over broccoli.

Makes 3 to 4 servings

12 ounces fresh broccoli, cut into florets with 2- or 3-inch stems
8 ounces processed cheese, cubed
3 tablespoons milk
½ teaspoon Worcestershire sauce (optional)

Double Cheddar Bacon Mashed Potatoes

Prep Time: 10 minutes • **Cook Time:** 20 minutes

1. In 3-quart saucepan, cover potatoes with water. Bring to a boil over high heat. Reduce heat to low and simmer uncovered 15 minutes or until potatoes are very tender; drain. Return potatoes to saucepan. Mash potatoes.

2. Stir Double Cheddar Sauce into mashed potatoes. Stir in bacon and salt.

Makes 6 servings

Tip: Stir in ¼ cup chopped green onions for an extra flavor boost.

2 pounds all-purpose potatoes, peeled and sliced
1 jar (1 pound) RAGÚ® Cheesy!® Double Cheddar Sauce, heated
5 slices bacon, crisp-cooked and crumbled (about ¼ cup)
1 teaspoon salt

Chutney'd Squash Circles

2 acorn squash (1 pound each)
2 tablespoons butter or margarine
½ cup prepared chutney

1. Preheat oven to 400°F. Slice tip and stem end from squash. Cut squash crosswise into ¾-inch rings. Scoop out and discard seeds.

2. Tear off 18-inch square of heavy-duty foil. Center foil in 13×9-inch baking dish. Dot foil with butter; place squash on butter, slightly overlapping rings. Spoon chutney over slices; sprinkle with 2 tablespoons water.

3. Bring foil on long sides of pan together in center, folding over to make tight seam. Fold ends to form tight seal.

4. Bake 20 to 30 minutes until squash is fork-tender. Transfer to warm serving plate. Pour pan drippings over squash.

Makes 4 side-dish servings

Sweet & Tangy Coleslaw

Prep Time: 5 minutes • **Cook Time:** 0 minutes

1 small bag (16 ounces) shredded cabbage
½ cup mayonnaise
½ cup *French's®* Honey Mustard

1. Combine ingredients in large bowl until blended.

2. Chill until ready to serve.

Makes 6 to 8 servings

3
ingredients

Salsa Macaroni & Cheese

Prep Time: 5 minutes • **Cook Time:** 15 minutes

1 jar (1 pound) RAGÚ®
    Cheesy! Double
    Cheddar Sauce
1 cup prepared mild salsa
8 ounces elbow macaroni,
    cooked and drained

1. In 2-quart saucepan, heat Double Cheddar Sauce over medium heat. Stir in salsa; heat through.

2. Toss with hot macaroni. Serve immediately.   *Makes 4 servings*

Oven-Roasted Asparagus

1 pound asparagus
2 tablespoons I CAN'T
    BELIEVE IT'S NOT
    BUTTER!® Spread,
    melted
2 cloves garlic, finely
    chopped
    Salt and black pepper to
    taste

Preheat oven to 425°F.

In large bowl, combine all ingredients. In 1½-quart baking dish, arrange asparagus mixture. Roast 20 minutes or until asparagus are tender. Garnish, if desired, with grated lemon peel and serve with lemon wedges.   *Makes 4 servings*

Note: Recipe can be halved.

Original Ranch® Roasted Potatoes

2 pounds small red
  potatoes, quartered
¼ cup vegetable oil
1 packet (1 ounce)
  HIDDEN VALLEY® The
  Original Ranch® Salad
  Dressing & Seasoning
  Mix

Place potatoes in a gallon-size Glad® Zipper Storage Bag. Pour oil over potatoes. Seal bag and toss to coat. Add salad dressing & seasoning mix; seal bag and toss again until coated. Bake in an ungreased baking pan at 450°F for 30 to 35 minutes or until potatoes are brown and crisp.   *Makes 4 to 6 servings*

Garlic Green Beans

Prep Time: 3 minutes • **Cook Time:** 5 to 10 minutes

1 package (16 ounces)
  frozen cut green beans,
  cooked according to
  package directions and
  drained
1 tablespoon I CAN'T
  BELIEVE IT'S NOT
  BUTTER!® Spread
1 teaspoon LAWRY'S®
  Garlic Salt

In medium bowl, gently toss hot beans to thoroughly coat and season with Spread and Garlic Salt.   *Makes 6 servings*

3 Marvelous Main Dishes ingredients

Garlic Pork Chops

Prep Time: 5 minutes • **Cook Time:** 25 minutes

6 bone-in pork chops,
¾ inch thick
1 envelope LIPTON®
RECIPE SECRETS®
Savory Herb with
Garlic Soup Mix
2 tablespoons vegetable oil
½ cup hot water

1. Preheat oven to 425°F. In broiler pan, without rack, arrange chops. Brush both sides of chops with soup mix blended with oil.

2. Bake chops 25 minutes or until done.

3. Remove chops to serving platter. Add hot water to pan and stir, scraping brown bits from bottom of pan. Serve sauce over chops.

Makes 4 servings

Old-Fashioned Turkey Pot Pie

1 package (18 ounces)
JENNIE-O TURKEY
STORE® SO EASY
Turkey Breast Chunks
In Homestyle Gravy
1½ cups frozen mixed
vegetables, thawed
⅛ teaspoon black pepper
1 package (15 ounces)
refrigerated pie crust,
divided

Preheat oven to 350°F.

In large bowl, combine turkey breast chunks in gravy, vegetables and pepper.

Place one pie crust in bottom and up side of 9-inch pie plate. Spoon turkey and vegetable mixture over crust. Place top crust over filling. Fold edges of crust inward and flute as desired to seal.

Bake 50 to 55 minutes or until crust is golden brown.

Cut into wedges to serve.

Makes 4 servings

Cranberry-Onion Pork Roast

1 boneless pork loin roast
(about 2 pounds)
1 can (16 ounces) whole
cranberry sauce
1 package (1 ounce) dry
onion soup mix

Season roast with salt and pepper; place over indirect heat on grill. Stir together cranberry sauce and onion soup mix in small microwavable bowl. Heat, covered, in microwave until hot, about 1 minute. Baste roast with cranberry mixture every 10 minutes until roast is done (internal temperature with a meat thermometer is 155° to 160°F), about 30 to 45 minutes. Let roast rest about 5 to 8 minutes before slicing to serve. Heat any leftover basting mixture to boiling; stir and boil for 5 minutes. Serve alongside roast.

Makes 4 to 6 servings

Favorite recipe from **National Pork Board**

Easy Sunday Dinner Roast Chicken

1 PERDUE® OVEN
   STUFFER® Roaster
   (5 to 7 pounds)
1 tablespoon olive or
   vegetable oil
1 package (about
   1¾ pounds) frozen
   Parmesan-herb-
   flavored vegetable
   mixture (potatoes,
   broccoli, cauliflower
   and carrots)

Preheat oven to 350°F. Remove giblets from chicken and reserve for another use. Rinse chicken under cold water and pat dry with paper towels. Rub skin with oil and season inside and out with 1 tablespoon of seasoning packet from vegetables. Place chicken in shallow roasting pan. Roast 2 to 2½ hours or until BIRD-WATCHER® Thermometer pops up and meat thermometer inserted into thickest part of thigh registers 180°F. During last 30 minutes of roasting time, arrange vegetables in pan around chicken and sprinkle with remaining seasonings. Before serving, remove and discard BIRD-WATCHER® Thermometer. Serve with vegetables. *Makes 6 servings*

Smothered Mozzarella Sandwiches

Prep Time: 5 minutes • **Cook Time:** 10 minutes

4 hero rolls, halved
   lengthwise
1 package (8 ounces)
   mozzarella cheese,
   sliced
1 cup RAGÚ® Organic Pasta
   Sauce, heated

1. Preheat oven to 425°F. On baking sheet, arrange rolls. Place cheese on bottom halves of rolls.

2. Bake 10 minutes or until cheese is melted and rolls are lightly toasted. Evenly spoon Pasta Sauce over cheese. Serve, if desired, with additional heated Pasta Sauce for dipping.
Makes 4 servings

Bronzed Fish

Place a heavy skillet over medium-high heat until hot, about 7 minutes.

As soon as skillet is hot, lightly coat one side of each fillet with butter, then sprinkle each buttered side evenly with ½ teaspoon of the seasoning of your choice. Place the fish in skillet, seasoned sides down, and sprinkle the top sides of all the fillets evenly with the remaining seasoning.

Cook until the undersides of the fillets are bronze in color, about 2½ minutes. Watch as the fish cooks and you'll see a white line coming up the side of each fillet as it turns from translucent to opaque; when one half of the thickness is opaque, the fish is ready to be turned. Turn the fish and cook approximately 2½ minutes longer. To test for doneness, simply touch the fish in the center; properly cooked fish will have a stiffer texture than partially cooked fish. You can also use a fork to flake the fish at its thickest part; if it flakes easily, it is done. **Do not overcook** as the fish will continue to cook even after you remove it from the heat. Serve immediately.

Makes 4 servings

Note: You can turn the fish more than once or continuously until cooked to desired doneness. All cooking times are approximate.

3 tablespoons unsalted butter, melted
4 (4½-ounce) fish fillets, each about ½ to ¾ inch thick at thickest part
About 1 tablespoon plus 1 teaspoon Chef Paul Prudhomme's Seafood Magic®, Chef Paul Prudhomme's Blackened Redfish Magic®, or Chef Paul Prudhomme's Meat Magic®

Mahogany Chops

Season chops with salt and black pepper; grill over medium-hot coals, basting with teriyaki and molasses. (Do not baste during last 5 minutes of grilling.)

Makes 4 servings

Favorite recipe from **National Pork Board**

4 top loin pork chops
6 tablespoons teriyaki sauce
2 tablespoons molasses (or ketchup)

3 ingredients

BBQ Roast Beef

2 pounds boneless cooked
    roast beef
1 bottle (12 ounces)
    barbecue sauce
10 to 12 sandwich rolls,
    halved

SLOW COOKER DIRECTIONS

1. Combine roast beef, barbecue sauce and 1½ cups water in slow cooker. Cover; cook on LOW 2 hours.

2. To serve, shred roast beef with 2 forks; place on rolls.

Makes 10 to 12 sandwiches

Grilled Tequila Lime Salmon

Prep Time: 5 minutes • **Marinate Time:** 30 minutes • **Cook Time:** 8 to 10 minutes

1 cup LAWRY'S® Tequila
    Lime Marinade with
    Lime Juice, divided
1 pound fresh salmon fillets
    or steaks
1 lime, cut into wedges
    Fresh cilantro sprigs
    (optional garnish)

In large resealable plastic bag, combine ¾ cup Tequila Lime Marinade and salmon; seal bag. Marinate in refrigerator for 30 minutes, turning occasionally. Remove salmon from bag, discarding used marinade. Grill salmon until opaque and fish begins to flake easily, 8 to 10 minutes, brushing often with remaining ¼ cup Marinade. Serve with lime wedges and fresh cilantro for garnish, if desired. *Makes 4 servings*

Serving Suggestion: Serve with black beans, rice and warm tortillas.

helpful hint:

Cleanup is easier if the grill rack is coated with vegetable oil or nonstick cooking spray before grilling. However, do not spray the cooking spray on the grill rack while it is over the fire as this could cause a flare-up.

Easy Family Burritos

1 boneless beef chuck
　　shoulder roast (2 to
　　3 pounds)
1 jar (24 ounces) *or* 2 jars
　　(16 ounces each) salsa
　　Flour tortillas, warmed

SLOW COOKER DIRECTIONS

1. Place roast in slow cooker; top with salsa. Cover; cook on LOW 8 to 10 hours.

2. Remove beef from slow cooker. Shred beef with 2 forks. Return to slow cooker. Cover; cook 1 to 2 hours or until heated through.

3. Serve shredded beef wrapped in warm tortillas.

Makes 8 servings

Serving Suggestion: Serve these tasty burritos with any combination of toppings, such as shredded cheese, sour cream, salsa, lettuce, tomato, onion or guacamole.

Penne with Red Pepper Alfredo Sauce

Prep Time: 20 minutes • **Cook Time:** 10 minutes

1 jar (7.25 ounces) roasted
　　red peppers, drained
1 jar (1 pound) RAGÚ®
　　Cheesy! Classic Alfredo
　　Sauce
8 ounces penne or ziti
　　pasta, cooked and
　　drained

1. In blender or food processor, purée roasted peppers.

2. In 2-quart saucepan, heat Alfredo Sauce over medium heat. Stir in puréed roasted peppers; heat through. Toss with hot pasta and garnish, if desired, with chopped fresh basil leaves.

Makes 4 servings

3
ingredients

Bow Ties with Vegetables Alfredo

Prep Time: 5 minutes • **Cook Time:** 20 minutes

1 package (8 ounces) bow tie pasta, uncooked
1 bag (16 ounces) BIRDS EYE® frozen Farm Fresh Mixtures Broccoli, Cauliflower & Carrots
1 package (1.6 ounces) alfredo pasta sauce mix
½ teaspoon black pepper

• In large saucepan, cook pasta according to package directions. Add vegetables during last 5 minutes of pasta cooking time. Drain; return to saucepan.

• Meanwhile, in medium saucepan, prepare sauce according to package directions.

• Stir sauce into vegetables and pasta; cook over medium heat until heated through.

• Season with pepper.

Makes 4 servings

Variation: Stir 2 tablespoons prepared pesto sauce into alfredo sauce.

Ranch Crispy Chicken

¼ cup unseasoned dry bread crumbs or cornflake crumbs
1 packet (1 ounce) HIDDEN VALLEY® The Original Ranch® Salad Dressing & Seasoning Mix
6 bone-in chicken pieces

Combine bread crumbs and salad dressing & seasoning mix in a gallon-size Glad® Zipper Storage Bag. Add chicken pieces; seal bag. Shake to coat chicken. Bake chicken on an ungreased baking pan at 375°F for 50 minutes or until no longer pink in center and juices run clear.

Makes 4 to 6 servings

Basic Fried Chicken

½ cup all-purpose flour
1 tablespoon seasoned salt
½ teaspoon black pepper
1 chicken, cut into pieces
Vegetable oil for frying

Combine flour, salt and pepper in gallon size plastic resealable food storage bag. Rinse chicken under cold running water; do not dry. Drop chicken, 2 to 3 pieces at a time, into flour mixture; shake to coat well. Heat ½ inch oil in large skillet over medium-high heat until hot. Place chicken, skin side down, in skillet. Turn pieces to brown evenly on all sides. Reduce heat to medium-low; cover and cook about 30 minutes or until fork can be inserted into chicken with ease and juices run clear, not pink. Drain on paper towels. Serve hot or cold. *Makes 4 servings*

Variations: Add 1 teaspoon dry mustard and 1 teaspoon dried thyme or 1 teaspoon curry powder *or* ½ teaspoon lemon pepper and ½ teaspoon dried thyme to flour mixture. Continue as directed.

Favorite recipe from **National Chicken Council**

Double Cheddar Sloppy Joes

Prep Time: 5 minutes • **Cook Time:** 10 minutes

1½ pounds ground beef
1 jar (1 pound) RAGÚ®
Cheesy!® Double
Cheddar Sauce
8 hamburger buns

1. In 12-inch nonstick skillet, brown ground beef over medium-high heat; drain.

2. Stir in Double Cheddar Sauce and heat through. Serve on hamburger buns. *Makes 8 servings*

Tip: To make Tex-Mex Style Sloppy Joes, stir in 1 tablespoon chili powder.

Hickory BBQ Chicken

1. Reserve ½ cup sauce to serve over cooked chicken; cover and refrigerate until 30 minutes before serving. Stir lime juice into remaining sauce in can. Arrange chicken in 11×7-inch dish. Cover with sauce mixture from can; turn to coat. Cover and refrigerate at least 30 minutes or overnight.

2. Grill chicken over hot coals (or broil) 4 minutes per side or until no longer pink in center, brushing chicken occasionally with marinade. Serve with reserved ½ cup sauce. (Any remaining marinade must be boiled for several minutes before serving with chicken.)

Makes 4 servings

1 can (15 ounces) DEL MONTE® BBQ Sloppy Joe Sauce
¼ cup fresh lime juice
4 boneless skinless chicken breast halves

Onion-Marinated Steak

Cut 1 onion in half; refrigerate one half. Chop remaining onion to equal 1½ cups. In blender or food processor, process 1 cup Wish-Bone Italian Dressing and chopped onion until puréed.

In large, shallow nonaluminum baking dish or plastic bag, pour 1¾ cups dressing-onion marinade over steak; turn to coat. Cover, or close bag, and marinate in refrigerator, turning occasionally, 3 to 24 hours. Refrigerate remaining ½ cup marinade.

Remove steak from marinade, discarding marinade. Grill or broil steak, turning and brushing frequently with refrigerated marinade, until steak is done.

Meanwhile, in saucepan, heat remaining 2 tablespoons Italian dressing and cook remaining onion half, cut into thin rings, stirring occasionally, 4 minutes or until tender. Serve over steak.

Makes 8 servings

2 large red onions
1 cup plus 2 tablespoons WISH-BONE® Italian Dressing*
1 (2- to 3-pound) boneless sirloin or London broil steak

Also terrific with Wish-Bone® Robusto Italian or Just 2 Good! Italian Dressing.

3
ingredients

Easy Skillet Ravioli

Prep Time: 5 minutes • **Cook Time:** 20 minutes

1 package (about
26 ounces) frozen
cheese ravioli
2¼ cups water
½ teaspoon salt
1 jar (1 pound 10 ounces)
RAGÚ® Chunky Pasta
Sauce
¼ cup heavy cream, half
and half, evaporated
milk, milk or nondairy
creamer (optional)

1. In 12-inch nonstick skillet, bring ravioli, water and salt to a boil over high heat. Continue boiling, stirring gently to separate ravioli, 5 minutes.

2. Stir in Pasta Sauce. Cook covered over medium heat, stirring occasionally, 10 minutes or until ravioli are tender. Stir in cream and heat through. Garnish, if desired, with grated Parmesan cheese.

Makes 4 servings

Honey Mustard Pecan Chicken

Prep Time: 10 minutes • **Cook Time:** 20 minutes

4 boneless skinless chicken
breast halves
¼ cup *French's®* Honey
Mustard
1 cup finely chopped
pecans

1. Preheat oven to 400°F. Spread mustard evenly on chicken. Coat with pecans, pressing gently to adhere.

2. Place chicken in greased and foil-lined baking pan. Bake 20 minutes or until chicken is no longer pink in center. Serve with additional mustard.

Makes 4 servings

3 Irresistible Goodies

ingredients

Toffee Chipsters

1 package (18 ounces)
   refrigerated sugar
   cookie dough
1 cup white chocolate
   chips
1 bag (8 ounces) chocolate-
   covered toffee baking
   bits, divided

1. Preheat oven to 350°F. Lightly grease cookie sheets. Let dough stand at room temperature about 15 minutes.

2. Combine dough, white chocolate chips and 1 cup toffee bits in large bowl; beat until well blended. Drop dough by rounded tablespoonfuls 2 inches apart onto prepared cookie sheets. Press remaining ⅓ cup toffee bits into dough mounds.

3. Bake 10 to 12 minutes or until set. Cool on cookie sheets 1 minute. Remove to wire racks; cool completely.

Makes about 2 dozen cookies

3 ingredients

Chocolate Peanut Butter Ice Cream Sandwiches

2 tablespoons creamy
   peanut butter
8 chocolate wafer cookies
⅔ cup vanilla ice cream,
   softened

1. Spread peanut butter over flat sides of all cookies.

2. Spoon ice cream over peanut butter on 4 cookies. Top with remaining 4 cookies, peanut butter sides down. Press down lightly to force ice cream to edges of sandwiches.

3. Wrap each sandwich tightly in foil. Freeze at least 2 hours or up to 5 days.

Makes 4 servings

White Chocolate Pecan Corn

1 pop & serve bag
   (3.5 ounces) JOLLY
   TIME® Butter-Licious or
   Crispy 'n White
   Microwave Pop Corn,
   popped
8 ounces vanilla flavored
   candy coating (white
   chocolate) *or*
   1 package (10 ounces)
   large vanilla flavored
   baking chips
½ cup pecan halves

Place popped popcorn in large bowl. Place candy coating in 1-quart glass measuring cup. Microwave on HIGH 1 to 1½ minutes, or until candy coating is shiny; stir to melt completely. Stir in pecans. Add mixture to popcorn and mix well. Spread on cookie sheet; allow to cool completely.

Makes about 2 quarts

Note: One pop & serve (3.5-ounce) package JOLLY TIME® Microwave Pop Corn yields about 12 cups popped popcorn.

Rockin' Raspberry Refresher

½ cup fresh or thawed
    frozen unsweetened
    raspberries
¼ cup frozen pink
    lemonade concentrate
2 cups club soda, chilled,
    divided

1. Place raspberries and lemonade concentrate in blender. Cover; blend on high speed until smooth. Add ½ cup club soda to blender; cover and blend until mixed.

2. Pour remaining 1½ cups club soda into small pitcher. Add raspberry mixture; stir. Pour into glasses; serve immediately.

Makes 2 servings

Dessert Grape Clusters

2 pounds seedless red
    and/or green grapes
1 pound premium white
    chocolate, coarsely
    chopped
2 cups finely chopped
    honey-roasted cashews

1. Rinse grapes under cold running water in colander; drain well. Cut grapes into clusters of 3 grapes. Place clusters in single layer on paper towels. Let stand at room temperature until completely dry.

2. Melt white chocolate in top of double boiler over hot, not boiling, water. Stir until white chocolate is melted. Remove from heat.

3. Place cashews in shallow bowl. Working with 1 cluster at a time, holding by stem, dip grapes into melted chocolate; allow excess to drain back into pan. Roll grapes gently in cashews. Place grapes, stem sides up, on waxed paper; repeat with remaining clusters. Refrigerate until firm. Serve within 4 hours.

Makes about 3 dozen clusters

Double Peanut Clusters

1²/₃ cups (10-ounce package)
        REESE'S® Peanut Butter
        Chips
    1 tablespoon shortening
        (do not use butter,
        margarine, spread or
        oil)
    2 cups salted peanuts

1. Line cookie sheet with wax paper.

2. Place peanut butter chips and shortening in large microwave-safe bowl. Microwave at HIGH (100%) 1½ minutes; stir until chips are melted and mixture is smooth. If necessary, microwave an additional 30 seconds until chips are melted when stirred. Stir in peanuts.

3. Drop by rounded teaspoons onto prepared cookie sheet. (Mixture may also be dropped into small paper candy cups.) Cool until set. Store in cool, dry place.   *Makes about 2½ dozen clusters*

Butterscotch Nut Clusters: Follow above directions, substituting 1¾ cups (11-ounce package) HERSHEY'S Butterscotch Chips for Peanut Butter Chips.

Easy Raspberry Ice Cream

1¾ cups frozen unsweetened
        raspberries
    2 to 3 tablespoons
        powdered sugar
    ½ cup whipping cream

1. Place raspberries in food processor fitted with steel blade. Process using on/off pulses about 15 seconds or until raspberries are finely chopped.

2. Add sugar; process using on/off pulses until smooth. With processor running, add cream; process until well blended. Serve immediately.   *Makes 3 servings*

3
ingredients

Zucchini-Orange Bread

1 package (about
    17 ounces) cranberry-
    orange muffin mix
1½ cups shredded zucchini
    (about 6 ounces)
1 teaspoon ground
    cinnamon
1 teaspoon freshly grated
    orange peel (optional)

1. Preheat oven to 350°F. Grease 8×4-inch loaf pan; set aside.

2. Combine muffin mix, zucchini, 1 cup water, cinnamon and orange peel, if desired, in medium bowl; stir just until dry ingredients are moistened. Spoon batter into prepared loaf pan; bake 40 minutes or until toothpick inserted into center comes out almost clean.

3. Cool in pan on wire rack 5 minutes. Remove bread from pan to wire rack; cool completely.   *Makes about 16 slices*

Serving Suggestion: Serve with cream cheese, if desired.

Milk Chocolate Pots de Crème

2 cups (11½-ounce
    package) HERSHEY'S
    Milk Chocolate Chips
½ cup light cream
½ teaspoon vanilla extract
    Sweetened whipped
    cream (optional)

1. Place milk chocolate chips and light cream in medium microwave-safe bowl. Microwave at HIGH (100%) 1 minute or just until chips are melted and mixture is smooth when stirred. Stir in vanilla.

2. Pour into demitasse cups or very small dessert dishes. Cover; refrigerate until firm. Serve cold with sweetened whipped cream, if desired.   *Makes 6 to 8 servings*

3
ingredients

Apple-Gingerbread Mini Cakes

Prep and Cook Time: 20 minutes

1 large Cortland or
   Jonathan apple, cored
   and quartered
1 package (14½ ounces)
   gingerbread cake and
   cookie mix
1 egg

MICROWAVE DIRECTIONS

1. Lightly grease 10 (6-ounce) microwavable custard cups; set aside. Grate apple in food processor or with hand-held grater.

2. Combine grated apple, cake mix, 1 cup water and egg in medium bowl; stir until well blended. Spoon about ⅓ cup batter into each custard cup, filling cups half full.

3. Arrange 5 cups in microwave. Microwave on HIGH 2 minutes. Rotate cups ½ turn. Microwave 1 minute more or until cakes are springy when touched and look slightly moist on top. Cool on wire rack. Repeat with remaining cakes.

4. To unmold cakes, while still warm run small knife around edges of custard cups to loosen. Invert onto cutting board and tap lightly until cake drops out. Place on plates. When cool enough, sprinkle with powdered sugar, if desired. Serve warm or at room temperature. *Makes 10 mini cakes*

Serving Suggestion: Serve with vanilla ice cream, whipped cream or crème anglaise.

helpful hint:

A four-sided box-shaped grater is a versatile and inexpensive tool that has several different size openings for grating hard ingredients. Graters that are flat sheets of metal with similar openings and a wire handle are also available. These often come in sets.

Passionate Sorbet

2 cups MAUNA LA'I®
  Paradise Passion® Juice
  Drink
¼ cup sugar
½ envelope of unflavored
  gelatin

1. Combine Mauna La'i Paradise Passion Juice Drink and sugar in medium saucepan. Sprinkle gelatin over juice drink and let sit 1 to 2 minutes to soften. Cook on low heat until gelatin and sugar dissolve, stirring occasionally. Pour into 9×9-inch pan and freeze until just firm.

2. Remove from freezer and cut into small pieces. Place frozen pieces in food processor. Process until light and creamy. Return to pan. Cover and freeze until firm. To serve, scrape off thin layers with spoon. *Makes 6 servings*

Fruit Medley Dessert

1 package (18 ounces)
  NESTLÉ® TOLL HOUSE®
  Refrigerated Mini Sugar
  Cookie Bar Dough
1 container (32 ounces)
  lowfat vanilla yogurt *or*
  1 quart vanilla frozen
  yogurt
4 cups fresh fruit
  (blueberries,
  raspberries, sliced
  apples, cherries,
  nectarines, peaches
  and/or strawberries)

PREHEAT oven to 325°F.

ROLL chilled dough on floured surface to ¼-inch thickness. Cut out 24 shapes using 3-inch cookie cutters. Place on ungreased baking sheets.

BAKE for 10 to 14 minutes or until edges are light golden brown. Cool on baking sheets for 2 minutes; remove to wire racks to cool completely.

PLACE two cookies on each plate. Top with ½ cup yogurt and ½ cup fruit mixture. Place third cookie on top. *Makes 8 servings*

Angel Almond Cupcakes

1 package DUNCAN
   HINES® Angel Food
   Cake Mix
1¼ cups water
2 teaspoons almond extract
1 container DUNCAN
   HINES® Wild Cherry
   Vanilla Frosting

1. Preheat oven to 350°F.

2. Combine cake mix, water and almond extract in large bowl. Beat at low speed with electric mixer until moistened. Beat at medium speed for 1 minute. Line medium muffin pans with paper baking cups. Fill muffin cups two-thirds full. Bake for 20 to 25 minutes or until golden brown, cracked and dry on top. Remove from muffin pans. Cool completely. Frost with frosting.

Makes 30 to 32 cupcakes

O.J. Yogurt Shake

1 cup 2% low-fat milk
1 carton (8 ounces) plain or
   vanilla low-fat yogurt
1 can (6 ounces) frozen
   orange juice
   concentrate
2 cups ice cubes, cracked

Add milk, yogurt and orange juice concentrate to food processor or blender. Process until smooth and frothy. Add ice; process until smooth and frothy.

Makes 5 (1-cup) servings

Favorite recipe from **Wisconsin Milk Marketing Board**

Chocolate Macadamia Chippers

1 package (18 ounces)
    refrigerated chocolate
    chip cookie dough
3 tablespoons unsweetened
    cocoa powder
½ cup coarsely chopped
    macadamia nuts

1. Preheat oven to 375°F. Let dough stand at room temperature about 15 minutes.

2. Combine dough and cocoa in large bowl; beat until well blended. (Dough may be kneaded lightly, if desired.) Stir in nuts. Drop by heaping tablespoons 2 inches apart onto ungreased cookie sheets.

3. Bake 9 to 11 minutes or until almost set. Transfer to wire racks to cool completely.

Makes 2 dozen cookies

Apple Yogurt Trifle

1 Washington Granny
    Smith apple, cored and
    finely chopped
2 (8-ounce) containers
    low-fat cherry yogurt
10 tablespoons crunchy
    nutlike cereal nuggets

Evenly divide half the chopped apple pieces among four parfait dishes or tall glasses. Divide yogurt from one 8-ounce container among dishes. Add 2 tablespoons cereal to each trifle, then top with layers of remaining yogurt, chopped apple and a sprinkle of cereal on top. Refrigerate at least 15 to 20 minutes before serving to allow cereal to soften slightly.

Makes 4 servings

Favorite recipe from ***Washington Apple Commission***

BelGioioso® Mascarpone Maple Syrup Sauce

8 ounces BELGIOIOSO®
Mascarpone
¼ cup pure maple syrup
Fresh peaches, pears,
strawberries,
blueberries, kiwi

Combine BelGioioso Mascarpone with maple syrup. Stir until mixture is smooth. (Maple syrup may be added to individual taste and consistency.) Drizzle sauce over arranged freshly cut fruit.

Thai Coconut Iced Tea

2 bags jasmine tea
2 tablespoons sugar
1 cup light coconut milk

1. Brew jasmine tea with 2 cups boiling water according to package directions; stir in sugar until dissolved. Let tea cool to room temperature.

2. Pour ½ cup coconut milk into each glass. Add ice; carefully pour half of tea into each glass. Serve immediately.

Makes 2 servings

helpful hint:

For a more dramatic presentation, gently pour the tea over the back of a spoon held close to the surface of the coconut milk. The tea will pool in a layer on top of the coconut milk before blending.

Chilled Café Latte

2 tablespoons instant coffee
¾ cup warm water
1 (14-ounce) can EAGLE BRAND® Fat Free or Original Sweetened Condensed Milk (NOT evaporated milk)
1 teaspoon vanilla extract
4 cups ice cubes

1. Dissolve coffee in water in blender container. Add EAGLE BRAND® and vanilla; blend on high speed until well blended.

2. Gradually add ice to blender, blending until smooth. Serve immediately. Store leftovers covered in refrigerator.

Makes 4 servings or about 5 cups latte

Easy Fruit Parfaits

Prep Time: 5 minutes • **Chill Time:** 4 hours

1 cup boiling water
1 package (4-serving size) gelatin, any red flavor
1 cup cold water
Frozen nondairy whipped topping, thawed
1 can (15.25 ounces) DOLE® Tropical Fruit Salad, drained

• Stir boiling water into gelatin in medium bowl 2 minutes until completely dissolved. Stir in cold water. Pour gelatin into 4 tall dessert or parfait glasses, filling about half full.

• Refrigerate 4 hours or until firm. To serve, layer with whipped topping and tropical fruit salad.

Makes 4 servings

Hugs® & Kisses® Crescents

1 package (8 ounces)
   refrigerated crescent
   dinner rolls
24 HERSHEY'S KISSES®
   Brand Milk Chocolates
   or HERSHEY'S HUGS®
   Chocolates
   Powdered sugar

1. Heat oven to 375°F. Separate dough into 8 triangles. Remove wrappers from chocolates.

2. Place 3 chocolates at center of wide end of each triangle (chocolates on each piece of dough should be touching one another). Starting at wide end, roll to opposite point; pinch edges to seal. Place rolls, pointed side down, on ungreased cookie sheet. Curve into crescent shape.

3. Bake 10 minutes or until lightly browned. Cool slightly; sprinkle with powdered sugar. Serve warm.   *Makes 8 crescents*

Note: Leftover crescents can be reheated in the microwave for a few seconds.

4
ingredients.....................................

4 ingredients

Table of Contents

4 Delicious Beginnings

ingredients

Cheese Straws

½ cup (1 stick) butter,
   softened
⅛ teaspoon salt
   Dash ground red pepper
1 pound sharp Cheddar
   cheese, shredded, at
   room temperature
2 cups self-rising flour

Heat oven to 350°F. In mixer bowl, beat butter, salt and pepper until creamy. Add cheese; mix well. Gradually add flour, mixing until dough begins to form a ball. Shape dough into ball with hands. Fit cookie press with desired plate; fill with dough according to manufacturer's directions. Press dough onto cookie sheets in 3-inch-long strips (or desired shapes). Bake 12 minutes or just until lightly browned. Cool completely on wire racks. Store tightly covered. *Makes about 10 dozen straws*

Favorite recipe from **Southeast United Dairy Industry Association, Inc.**

Fast Guacamole and "Chips"

2 ripe avocados
½ cup chunky salsa
¼ teaspoon hot pepper
   sauce
½ seedless cucumber, sliced
   into ⅛-inch-thick
   rounds

1. Cut avocados in half; remove and discard pits. Scoop flesh into medium bowl; mash with fork.

2. Add salsa and hot pepper sauce to avocados; mix well.

3. Transfer guacamole to serving bowl. Serve with cucumber "chips." *Makes 8 servings*

Festive Franks

1 can (8 ounces) crescent
   roll dough
5½ teaspoons barbecue sauce
⅓ cup finely shredded sharp
   Cheddar cheese
8 hot dogs
¼ teaspoon poppy seeds
   (optional)

1. Preheat oven to 350°F. Spray large baking sheet with nonstick cooking spray; set aside.

2. Unroll dough and separate into 8 triangles. Cut each triangle in half lengthwise to make 2 triangles. Lightly spread barbecue sauce over each triangle. Sprinkle with cheese.

3. Cut each hot dog in half; trim off rounded ends. Place one hot dog piece at large end of one dough triangle. Roll up jelly-roll style from wide end. Place point-side down on prepared baking sheet. Sprinkle with poppy seeds, if desired. Repeat with remaining hot dog pieces and dough.

4. Bake 13 minutes or until golden brown. Cool 1 to 2 minutes on baking sheet. Serve with additional barbecue sauce for dipping, if desired. *Makes 16 servings*

Asiago Pepper Shrimp

24 large Florida shrimp,
    peeled and deveined
8 ounces asiago cheese
1 tablespoon chopped
    Florida jalapeño pepper
12 slices bacon

Wash the shrimp and pat them dry. Butterfly shrimp by cutting lengthwise along the back (don't cut all the way through), leaving the tail section intact. Grate the cheese and mix with jalapeño pepper. Cut each piece of bacon in half. Fill the open section of each shrimp with about ⅛ teaspoon cheese mixture. Wrap each shrimp with a piece of bacon; secure with a wooden pick. Place shrimp on a broiler pan; broil until bacon is crisp. Turn the shrimp and broil until shrimp are opaque and bacon is done.

Makes 6 appetizers

Favorite recipe from **Florida Department of Agriculture and Consumer Services, Bureau of Seafood and Aquaculture**

Roast Beef Roll-Ups

2 tablespoons horseradish
    mayonnaise
2 slices deli roast beef
2 tablespoons crumbled
    blue cheese
    Red onion slices

1. Spread mayonnaise on roast beef slices. Sprinkle with blue cheese; layer with onion slices.

2. Roll up roast beef slices from short ends.

Makes 2 roll-ups

helpful hint:

When onions are cut, they release sulfur compounds that can bring tears to the eyes. Try one of these suggestions for minimizing tears: place the onion in the freezer for 20 minutes before slicing; chew a piece of bread while peeling and slicing; breathe through your nose and keep your mouth closed while slicing; work under an exhaust fan; work as quickly as possible, never touching your eyes.

ROAST BEEF ROLL-UPS

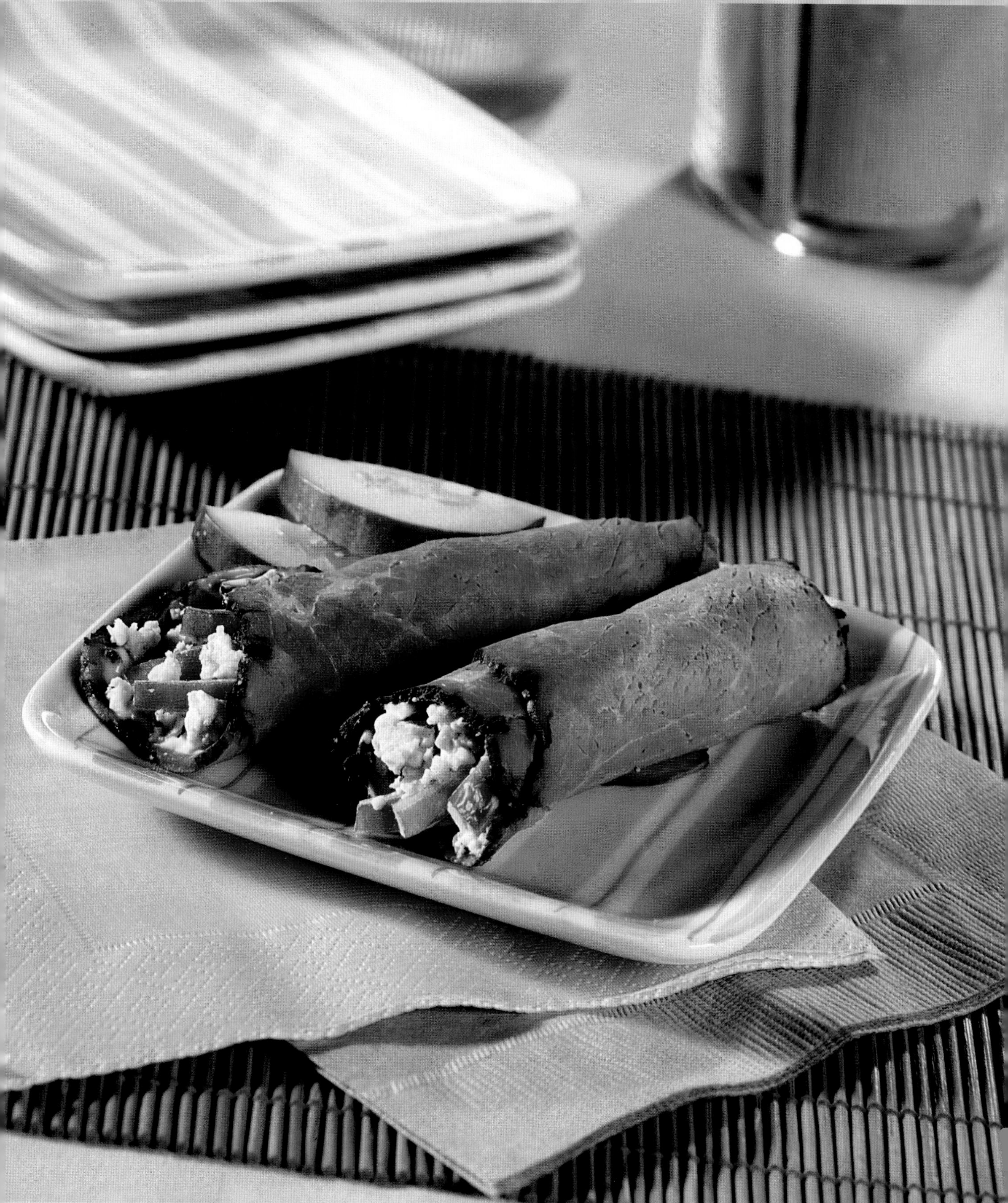

Pasta Snacks

4 ounces uncooked pasta
(wagon wheels, bowties
or cork screws)
Vegetable oil for deep
frying
2 tablespoons grated
Parmesan cheese
1 tablespoon ground
walnuts
$\frac{1}{8}$ teaspoon garlic salt

Cook pasta according to package directions; drain. Rinse in cold water and drain well. Spread cooked pasta on paper towels to remove additional water.

Heat 2 inches oil in deep fat fryer or deep saucepan to 400°F. Fry pasta, a few at a time, until golden, about 30 to 45 seconds. Remove with slotted spoon; drain thoroughly. Mix cheese, walnuts and garlic salt; toss with fried pasta. Store in airtight container.

Makes 2½ cups

Favorite recipe from **North Dakota Wheat Commission**

Beefy Bruschetta

Prep Time: 5 minutes • **Cook Time:** 10 minutes

1 loaf French or Italian
bread (about 16 inches
long), diagonally cut
into 1-inch slices
$\frac{1}{3}$ cup prepared pesto
1 cup RAGÚ® Rich & Meaty
Meat Sauce, heated
1 cup shredded mozzarella
cheese (about
4 ounces)

1. On ungreased baking sheet, arrange bread. Broil bread until golden, about 1 minute. Remove from oven.

2. Evenly spread pesto on bread, then evenly top with Meat Sauce and sprinkle with cheese. Broil until cheese is melted.

Makes 8 servings

Spinach Cheese Bundles

1 package (6½ ounces)
   garlic-and-herb
   spreadable cheese
½ cup chopped fresh
   spinach
1 package (17¼ ounces)
   frozen puff pastry
   dough, thawed
   Sweet-and-sour or other
   favorite dipping sauce

1. Preheat oven to 400°F. Combine cheese, spinach and ¼ teaspoon black pepper in small bowl; mix well.

2. Roll out 1 puff pastry sheet on floured surface into 12-inch square. Cut into 16 (3-inch) squares. Place about 1 teaspoon cheese mixture in center of each square. Brush edges of squares with water. Bring edges together over filling; twist tightly to seal. Fan out corners of puff pastry. Repeat with remaining puff pastry and cheese mixture.

3. Place bundles 2 inches apart on ungreased baking sheets. Bake about 13 minutes or until golden brown. Serve warm with dipping sauce.   *Makes 32 bundles*

Hot French Onion Dip

1 envelope LIPTON®
   RECIPE SECRETS®
   Onion Soup Mix
1 container (16 ounces)
   sour cream
2 cups shredded Swiss
   cheese (about
   8 ounces), divided
¼ cup HELLMANN'S® or
   BEST FOODS® Real
   Mayonnaise

1. Preheat oven to 375°F. In 1-quart casserole, combine soup mix, sour cream, 1¾ cups Swiss cheese and mayonnaise.

2. Bake uncovered 20 minutes or until heated through. Sprinkle with remaining ¼ cup cheese.

3. Serve, if desired, with sliced French bread or your favorite dippers.   *Makes 2 cups dip*

4

ingredients

Creamy Hot Artichoke Dip

Prep Time: 5 minutes • **Cook Time:** 25 minutes

1 can (14 ounces) artichoke hearts, drained and chopped
1 cup HELLMANN'S® or BEST FOODS® Real Mayonnaise
1 cup grated Parmesan cheese (about 4 ounces)
1 clove garlic, finely chopped *or* ¼ teaspoon LAWRY'S® Garlic Powder With Parsley (optional)

1. Preheat oven to 350°F.

2. In 1-quart casserole, combine all ingredients. Bake uncovered 25 minutes or until heated through. Serve with your favorite dippers.

Makes 2½ cups dip

Spinach & Artichoke Dip: Add 1 package (10 ounces) frozen chopped spinach, thawed and squeezed dry.

Seafood Artichoke Dip: Add 1 can (6 ounces) crabmeat, drained and flaked.

Italian Artichoke Dip: Add ½ cup shredded mozzarella cheese and ¼ cup drained and chopped sun-dried tomatoes.

Rainbow Spirals

Prep Time: 10 minutes

4 (10-inch) flour tortillas (assorted flavors and colors)
4 tablespoons *French's®* Mustard (any flavor)
½ pound (about 8 slices) thinly sliced deli roast beef, bologna or turkey
8 slices American, provolone or Muenster cheese
Fancy party toothpicks

1. Spread each tortilla with *1 tablespoon* mustard. Layer with meat and cheeses dividing evenly.

2. Roll up jelly-roll style; secure with toothpicks and cut into thirds. Arrange on platter.

Makes 4 to 6 servings

Pizza Dippin' Strips

Prep Time: 10 minutes • **Cook Time:** 15 minutes

1 package (13.8 ounces)
   refrigerated pizza crust
   dough
15 thin slices pepperoni
1 cup shredded mozzarella
   cheese (about
   4 ounces)
1 jar (1 pound 10 ounces)
   RAGÚ® Organic Pasta
   Sauce, heated

1. Preheat oven to 400°F.

2. On greased baking sheet, roll pizza dough into 12×9-inch rectangle. Fold edges over to make ¾-inch crust. Bake 7 minutes.

3. Evenly top pizza crust with pepperoni, then cheese. Bake an additional 8 minutes or until cheese is melted. Let stand 2 minutes.

4. Cut pizza in half lengthwise, then into 1½-inch strips. Serve with Pasta Sauce, heated, for dipping.   *Makes 16 strips*

Original Ranch® Meatballs

1 pound ground beef
1 packet (1 ounce)
   HIDDEN VALLEY® The
   Original Ranch® Salad
   Dressing & Seasoning
   Mix
2 tablespoons butter or
   margarine
½ cup beef broth

Combine ground beef and salad dressing & seasoning mix in a large bowl. Shape into meatballs. Melt butter in a skillet; brown meatballs on all sides. Add broth; cover and simmer 10 to 15 minutes or until cooked through. Serve warm with toothpicks.

Makes 2 dozen meatballs

Crostini

¼ loaf whole wheat
baguette (4 ounces)
4 plum tomatoes
1 cup (4 ounces) shredded
mozzarella cheese
3 tablespoons prepared
pesto

1. Preheat oven to 400°F. Slice baguette into 16 very thin, diagonal slices. Slice each tomato lengthwise into four ¼-inch slices.

2. Place baguette slices on ungreased nonstick baking sheet. Top each with 1 tablespoon cheese and 1 slice tomato. Bake about 8 minutes or until bread is lightly toasted and cheese is melted. Top each crostini with about ½ teaspoon pesto sauce. Serve warm.

Makes 8 appetizer servings

Pear Walnut Cheese Spread

1 can (15 ounces) Bartlett
pears, finely diced
½ cup toasted walnuts,
chopped
2 tablespoons chopped
chives
1 cup (4 ounces) crumbled
blue cheese

Combine pears, walnuts and chives in medium bowl. Stir in blue cheese. Serve as a dip with crackers or toasted pita bread triangles.

Makes 2 cups spread

Favorite recipe from *Pacific Northwest Canned Pear Service*

Baked Apricot Brie

Cook Time: 12 minutes

1 round (8 ounces) Brie
  cheese
⅓ cup apricot preserves
2 tablespoons sliced
  almonds
  Cracked pepper or other
  assorted crackers

1. Preheat oven to 400°F. Place cheese in small baking pan. Spread top of cheese with preserves; sprinkle with almonds.

2. Bake about 10 to 12 minutes or until cheese begins to melt and lose its shape. Serve hot with crackers. Refrigerate leftovers; reheat before serving.   *Makes 6 servings*

Notes: Brie is a soft-ripened, unpressed cheese made from cow's milk. It has a distinctive round shape, edible white rind and creamy yellow interior. Avoid Brie that has a chalky center (it is underripe) or a strong ammonia odor (it is overripe). The cheese should give slightly to pressure and have an evenly colored, barely moist rind.

Salsa Bean Dip

1 can (16 ounces)
  ORTEGA® Refried
  Beans
½ cup ORTEGA Salsa-Thick
  & Chunky
½ cup (2 ounces) shredded
  cheddar cheese
  Tortilla chips

HEAT beans, salsa and cheese in medium saucepan over medium-high heat for 3 to 4 minutes or until bubbly and cheese is melted. Serve with chips.   *Makes 6 to 8 servings*

Variation: Add ¼ cup ORTEGA® Diced Green Chiles or 2 teaspoons ORTEGA Diced Jalapenos.

Sausage Pinwheels

2 cups biscuit mix
½ cup milk
¼ cup (½ stick) butter or
    margarine, melted
1 pound BOB EVANS®
    Original Recipe Roll
    Sausage

Combine biscuit mix, milk and butter in large bowl until blended. Refrigerate 30 minutes. Divide dough into two portions. Roll out one portion on floured surface to ⅛-inch-thick rectangle, about 10×7 inches. Spread with half the sausage. Roll lengthwise into long roll. Repeat with remaining dough and sausage. Place rolls in freezer until firm enough to cut easily. Preheat oven to 400°F. Cut rolls into thin slices. Place on *ungreased* baking sheets. Bake 15 minutes or until golden brown. Serve hot. Refrigerate leftovers.

Makes 48 pinwheels

Note: This recipe can be doubled. Refreeze after slicing. When ready to serve, thaw slices in refrigerator and bake.

Potato Skins

4 baked potatoes,
    quartered
¼ cup sour cream
1 packet (1 ounce)
    HIDDEN VALLEY® The
    Original Ranch® Salad
    Dressing & Seasoning
    Mix
1 cup (4 ounces) shredded
    Cheddar cheese
    Sliced green onions
    and/or bacon pieces*
    (optional)

Scoop potato out of skins; combine potatoes, sour cream and salad dressing & seasoning mix in medium bowl. Fill skins with potato mixture. Sprinkle with cheese. Bake at 375°F for 12 to 15 minutes or until cheese is melted. Garnish with green onions and/or bacon bits, if desired.

Makes 8 to 10 servings

*Crisp-cooked, crumbled bacon can be used.

4 Incredible Side Dishes

ingredients

Roast Herbed Sweet Potatoes with Bacon & Onions

3 thick slices applewood-smoked or peppered bacon, diced

2 pounds sweet potatoes, peeled and cut into 2-inch chunks

2 medium onions, cut into 8 wedges

1 teaspoon dried thyme

1. Preheat oven to 375°F. Cook bacon in large, deep skillet until crisp. Remove from heat. Transfer bacon to paper towels; set aside. Add potatoes and onions to drippings in skillet; toss until coated. Stir in 1 teaspoon salt, thyme and ¼ teaspoon black pepper.

2. Spread mixture in single layer in ungreased 15×10-inch jelly-roll pan or shallow roasting pan. Bake 40 to 50 minutes or until golden brown and tender. Transfer to serving bowl; sprinkle with bacon. *Makes 10 to 12 servings*

Note: Potatoes can be prepared and baked up to 4 hours before serving; let stand at room temperature.

Peas with Cukes & Dill

2 pounds fresh peas*
2 tablespoons butter
½ medium cucumber,
    halved, seeded and cut
    into ¼-inch slices
1 teaspoon dried dill weed

*Or substitute 1 (10-ounce)
package frozen peas, thawed,
for fresh peas.*

1. Shell peas into colander; discard pods. Rinse peas under running water. Drain well; set aside.

2. Heat butter in medium skillet over medium-high heat until melted and bubbly. Cook and stir peas and cucumber in hot butter 5 minutes or until vegetables are crisp-tender.

3. Stir in dill weed; season with salt and black pepper to taste. Transfer to warm serving dish. Serve immediately.

Makes 4 servings

Quick Corn Bread with Chilies 'n' Cheese

1 package (12 to
    16 ounces) corn bread
    or corn muffin mix
1 cup (4 ounces) shredded
    Monterey Jack cheese,
    divided
1 can (4 ounces) chopped
    green chilies, drained
1 envelope LIPTON®
    RECIPE SECRETS®
    Vegetable Soup Mix

1. Prepare corn bread mix according to package directions; stir in ½ cup cheese, chilies and soup mix.

2. Spread batter in lightly greased 8-inch baking pan; bake as directed. While warm, top with remaining ½ cup cheese. Cool completely on wire rack. To serve, cut into squares.

Makes 16 servings

1-2-3 Cheddar Broccoli Casserole

Prep Time: 5 minutes • **Cook Time:** 20 minutes

1 jar (1 pound) RAGÚ®
  Cheesy!® Double
  Cheddar Sauce
2 boxes (10 ounces each)
  frozen broccoli florets,
  thawed
¼ cup plain or Italian
  seasoned dry bread
  crumbs
1 tablespoon I CAN'T
  BELIEVE IT'S NOT
  BUTTER!® Spread,
  melted

1. Preheat oven to 350°F. In 1½-quart casserole, combine Double Cheddar Sauce and broccoli.

2. Evenly top with bread crumbs combined with I Can't Believe It's Not Butter!® Spread.

3. Bake, uncovered, 20 minutes or until bread crumbs are golden and broccoli is tender. *Makes 6 servings*

Tip: Substitute your favorite frozen vegetables or vegetable blend for broccoli florets.

Wisconsin Cheese Pull-Apart Bread

3 packages (about 3 dozen)
  frozen bread dough
  dinner rolls, thawed to
  room temperature
⅓ cup butter, melted
1 cup freshly grated
  Wisconsin Parmesan
  cheese
1 cup shredded Wisconsin
  Provolone cheese

Roll each dinner roll in butter, then in Parmesan cheese to coat. Arrange half the rolls in well-greased 12-cup fluted tube pan. Sprinkle with Provolone cheese. Top with remaining rolls. Sprinkle with any remaining Parmesan cheese. Let rise about 1 hour or until doubled in bulk.

Preheat oven to 375°F. Bake 35 to 45 minutes or until golden brown. Use table knife to loosen edges of bread. Remove from pan. Serve warm. *Makes 12 servings*

Tip: Cover edges of bread with foil during last 10 to 15 minutes of baking if crust becomes too dark.

Favorite recipe from ***Wisconsin Milk Marketing Board***

Glazed Maple Acorn Squash

1 large acorn or golden
   acorn squash
2 tablespoons pure maple
   syrup
1 tablespoon butter, melted
¼ teaspoon ground
   cinnamon

1. Preheat oven to 375°F.

2. Cut stem and blossom ends from squash. Cut squash crosswise into 4 or 5 equal slices. Discard seeds and membrane. Place ¼ cup water in 13×9-inch baking dish. Arrange squash in dish; cover with foil. Bake 30 minutes or until tender.

3. Combine maple syrup, butter and cinnamon in small bowl; mix well. Uncover squash; pour off water. Brush squash with syrup mixture, letting excess pool in center of squash rings.

4. Return to oven; bake 10 minutes or until syrup mixture is bubbly.
Makes 4 to 5 servings

Sautéed Snow Peas
& Baby Carrots

1 tablespoon I CAN'T
   BELIEVE IT'S NOT
   BUTTER!® Spread
2 tablespoons chopped
   shallots or onion
5 ounces frozen whole
   baby carrots, partially
   thawed
4 ounces snow peas (about
   1 cup)
2 teaspoons chopped fresh
   parsley (optional)

In 12-inch nonstick skillet, melt I Can't Believe It's Not Butter!® Spread over medium heat and cook shallots, stirring occasionally, 1 minute or until almost tender. Add carrots and snow peas and cook, stirring occasionally, 4 minutes or until crisp-tender. Stir in parsley, if desired, and heat through.
Makes 2 servings

Note: Recipe can be doubled.

Original Green Bean Casserole

Prep Time: 5 minutes • **Cook Time:** 35 minutes

1 can (10¾ ounces)
    condensed cream of
    mushroom soup,
    undiluted
¾ cup milk
⅛ teaspoon black pepper
2 packages (9 ounces each)
    frozen cut green beans,
    thawed*
1⅓ cups *French's®* French
    Fried Onions, divided

**Substitute 2 cans (14½ ounces
each) cut green beans, drained,
for frozen green beans.*

1. Preheat oven to 350°F. Combine soup, milk and black pepper in 1½-quart casserole; stir until well blended. Stir in beans and ⅔ *cup* French Fried Onions.

2. Bake, uncovered, 30 minutes or until hot; stir. Sprinkle with remaining ⅔ *cup* onions. Bake 5 minutes or until onions are golden brown. *Makes 6 servings*

Microwave Directions: **Prepare green bean mixture as above in 1½-quart microwave-safe casserole. Cover with vented plastic wrap. Microwave on HIGH 8 to 10 minutes or until heated through, stirring halfway through cooking time. Uncover. Top with remaining onions. Cook 1 minute until onions are golden. Let stand 5 minutes.**

Garlic Mashed Potatoes

6 medium all-purpose
    potatoes, peeled, if
    desired, and cut into
    chunks (about
    3 pounds)
    Water
1 envelope LIPTON®
    RECIPE SECRETS®
    Savory Herb with
    Garlic Soup Mix*
½ cup milk
½ cup I CAN'T BELIEVE IT'S
    NOT BUTTER!® Spread

**Also terrific with LIPTON®
RECIPE SECRETS® Onion or
Golden Onion Soup Mix.*

1. In 4-quart saucepan, cover potatoes with water; bring to a boil.

2. Reduce heat to low and simmer uncovered 20 minutes or until potatoes are very tender; drain.

3. Return potatoes to saucepan, then mash. Stir in remaining ingredients. *Makes 8 servings*

Spinach Mediterranean Style

1 pound fresh spinach,
  washed, drained and
  stems removed
2 tablespoons FILIPPO
  BERIO® Olive Oil
1 clove garlic, minced
1 teaspoon balsamic or
  wine vinegar

MICROWAVE DIRECTIONS

Place spinach in microwave-safe 8- or 9-inch square baking dish. Drizzle with olive oil; sprinkle with garlic. Cover with vented plastic wrap. Microwave on HIGH (100% power) 5 minutes or until spinach is wilted, stirring halfway through cooking. Sprinkle with vinegar.

Makes 3 to 4 servings

Sweet & Tangy Marinated Vegetables

8 cups mixed fresh
  vegetables, such as
  broccoli, cauliflower,
  zucchini, carrots and
  red bell peppers, cut
  into 1- to 1½-inch
  pieces
⅓ cup distilled white
  vinegar
¼ cup sugar
¼ cup water
1 packet (1 ounce)
  HIDDEN VALLEY® The
  Original Ranch® Salad
  Dressing & Seasoning
  Mix

Place vegetables in a gallon-size Glad® Zipper Storage Bag. Combine vinegar, sugar, water and salad dressing & seasoning mix in a medium bowl. Whisk until sugar dissolves; pour over vegetables. Seal bag and shake to coat. Refrigerate 4 hours or overnight, turning bag occasionally.

Makes 8 servings

Note: Vegetables will keep up to 3 days in refrigerator.

Nutmeg & Honey Carrot Crescents

1 pound fresh carrots
⅓ cup water
2 tablespoons honey
¼ teaspoon freshly grated
  nutmeg
2 tablespoons chopped
  walnuts

1. Wash and peel carrots. To make carrot crescents, cut carrots in half lengthwise. Place cut sides down. Cut carrots into ¼-inch diagonal slices.

2. Place carrots and ⅓ cup water in large saucepan; cover. Bring to a boil over high heat; reduce heat to medium-low. Simmer carrots about 8 minutes or until fork-tender.

3. Transfer carrots with slotted spoon to warm serving dish. Bring remaining liquid in saucepan to a boil until liquid is almost evaporated. Add honey and nutmeg; stir. Toss honey mixture with carrots to coat. Sprinkle with walnuts. Serve immediately.

Makes 4 servings

Sherried Mushrooms

½ cup (1 stick) butter
1 cup HOLLAND HOUSE®
  Sherry Cooking Wine
1 clove garlic, crushed
18 fresh mushrooms, sliced

Melt butter in medium skillet over medium heat. Add cooking wine and garlic. Add mushrooms; cook until tender, about 5 minutes, stirring frequently. Season to taste with salt and black pepper.

Makes 2 to 3 servings

Frenched Beans with Celery

¾ pound fresh green beans, trimmed
2 stalks celery, cut diagonally into slices
2 tablespoons butter, melted
2 tablespoons toasted sunflower seeds*

*To toast sunflower seeds, heat ½ teaspoon oil in small skillet over medium heat. Add shelled sunflower seeds; cook and stir 3 minutes or until lightly browned, shaking pan constantly. Remove to paper towels.

1. Cut beans lengthwise; set aside.

2. Bring 1 inch of water in 2-quart saucepan to a boil over high heat. Add beans and celery. Cover; reduce heat to medium-low. Simmer 8 minutes or until beans are crisp-tender; drain.

3. Toss beans and celery with butter. Transfer to warm serving dish. Sprinkle with sunflower seeds. Serve immediately.

Makes 6 servings

Creamed Spinach

Prep Time: 5 minutes • **Cook Time:** 10 minutes

2 cups milk
1 package KNORR® Recipe Classics™ Leek recipe mix
1 bag (16 ounces) frozen chopped spinach
⅛ teaspoon ground nutmeg

• In medium saucepan, combine milk and recipe mix. Bring to a boil over medium heat.

• Add spinach and nutmeg; stirring frequently. Bring to a boil over high heat. Reduce heat to low and simmer, stirring frequently, 5 minutes.

Makes 6 servings

Holiday Vegetable Bake

Prep Time: 5 minutes • **Cook Time:** 10 minutes

1 package (16 ounces) frozen vegetable combination
1 can (10¾ ounces) condensed cream of broccoli soup, undiluted
⅓ cup milk
1⅓ cups *French's®* French Fried Onions, divided

MICROWAVE DIRECTIONS

1. Combine vegetables, soup, milk and ⅔ *cup* French Fried Onions in 2-quart microwavable casserole. Microwave,* uncovered, on HIGH 10 to 12 minutes or until vegetables are crisp-tender, stirring halfway through cooking time.

2. Sprinkle with remaining ⅔ *cup* onions. Microwave 1 minute or until onions are golden.   *Makes 4 to 6 servings*

**Or, bake in preheated 375°F oven 30 to 35 minutes.*

Easy Pineapple Slaw

Prep Time: 5 minutes

1 can (15¼ ounces) DEL MONTE® Pineapple Tidbits In Its Own Juice
⅓ cup mayonnaise
2 tablespoons vinegar
6 cups coleslaw mix or shredded cabbage

1. Drain pineapple, reserving 3 tablespoons juice.

2. Combine reserved juice, mayonnaise and vinegar; toss with pineapple and coleslaw mix. Season with salt and black pepper to taste, if desired.   *Makes 4 to 6 servings*

Roasted Idaho & Sweet Potatoes

1 envelope LIPTON®
   RECIPE SECRETS®
   Onion Soup Mix
2 medium all-purpose
   potatoes, peeled, if
   desired, and cut into
   large chunks (about
   1 pound)
2 medium sweet potatoes
   or yams, peeled, if
   desired, and cut into
   large chunks (about
   1 pound)
¼ cup BERTOLLI® Olive Oil

1. Preheat oven to 425°F. In large plastic bag or bowl, combine all ingredients. Close bag and shake, or toss in bowl, until potatoes are evenly coated.

2. In 13×9-inch baking or roasting pan, arrange potatoes; discard plastic bag.

3. Bake uncovered, stirring occasionally, 40 minutes or until potatoes are tender and golden.

Makes 4 servings

Cucumber Salad

2 cucumbers
½ cup plain nonfat yogurt
1 teaspoon dried mint
½ teaspoon sugar

Slice cucumbers. Combine yogurt, mint and sugar in small bowl. Toss cucumbers in yogurt mixture. Serve immediately.

Makes 4 servings

Favorite recipe from ***The Sugar Association, Inc.***

4 Main-Dish Delights

ingredients

2 cups fire-roasted diced
   tomatoes*
6 slices bacon, cut into
   1-inch pieces
4 pounds bone-in chicken
   pieces (about 8 pieces)
1 onion, cut into ⅓-inch
   slices

*Fire-roasted tomatoes give this
dish a deeper, more complex
flavor. Look for them in your
supermarket or specialty store
next to the other canned
tomato products.*

Baked Chicken
with Bacon-Tomato Sauce

1. Preheat oven to 450°F. Spread tomatoes in lightly greased
13×9-inch baking dish.

2. Cook bacon in large nonstick skillet over medium-high heat
until crisp, about 8 minutes, turning once. Drain on paper towels.
Reserve skillet and drippings.

3. Season chicken pieces with ½ teaspoon salt and ¼ teaspoon
black pepper. Cook chicken in another large skillet over high heat
until browned and crisp, about 5 minutes, turning as needed to
brown evenly. Arrange chicken over tomatoes. Bake, uncovered,
30 to 40 minutes or until chicken is no longer pink in center.

4. Meanwhile, cook onion in reserved bacon drippings until
golden, about 8 minutes. Transfer to brown paper bag with slotted
spoon. Add ¼ teaspoon salt; shake to degrease onions and mix
with salt.

5. Transfer chicken and tomatoes to serving plate; sprinkle with
bacon and onions. *Makes 4 servings*

Penne with Roasted Chicken & Vegetables

1 whole roasted chicken
   (about 2 pounds)
1 box (16 ounces) penne
   pasta
1 pound roasted vegetables,
   cut into bite-size pieces
1/3 cup shredded Parmesan
   cheese

1. Remove chicken meat from bones and shred. Discard bones and skin.

2. Cook pasta according to package directions; drain and return to hot cooking pot. Add chicken and vegetables; toss until heated through. Sprinkle with cheese and season with black pepper to taste.

Makes 6 servings

Nutty Pan-Fried Trout

2 tablespoons olive or
   vegetable oil
4 trout fillets (about
   6 ounces each)
1/2 cup seasoned bread
   crumbs
1/2 cup pine nuts

1. Heat oil in large skillet over medium heat. Lightly coat fish with bread crumbs. Add to skillet.

2. Cook 4 minutes on each side or until fish flakes easily when tested with fork. Remove fish from skillet. Place on serving platter; keep warm.

3. Add pine nuts to drippings in skillet. Cook and stir 3 minutes or until nuts are lightly toasted. Sprinkle over fish.

Makes 4 servings

Creamy Beef and Vegetable Casserole

Prep Time: 5 minutes • **Cook Time:** 10 to 15 minutes

1 pound lean ground beef
1 small onion, chopped
1 bag (16 ounces) BIRDS EYE® frozen Farm Fresh Mixtures Broccoli, Corn & Red Peppers
1 can (10¾ ounces) cream of mushroom soup, undiluted

• In medium skillet, brown beef and onion; drain excess fat.

• Meanwhile, in large saucepan, cook vegetables according to package directions; drain.

• Stir in beef mixture and soup. Cook over medium heat until heated through.

Makes 4 servings

Serving Suggestion: Serve over rice and sprinkle with ½ cup shredded Cheddar cheese.

Spanish Pork Chops

Prep Time: 5 minutes • **Cook Time:** 30 minutes

4 pork chops (about 1 pound)
1 (6.8-ounce) package RICE-A-RONI® Spanish Rice
2 tablespoons margarine or butter
1 (14½-ounce) can diced tomatoes, undrained

1. In large skillet over medium-high heat, brown pork chops 3 minutes on each side; set aside.

2. In same skillet, sauté rice-vermicelli with margarine until vermicelli is golden brown.

3. Slowly stir in 2¼ cups water, tomatoes and Special Seasonings; bring to a boil. Reduce heat to low. Cover; simmer 10 minutes.

4. Add pork chops; return to a simmer. Cover; simmer 8 to 10 minutes or until rice is tender and pork chops are no longer pink inside.

Makes 4 servings

Sweet & Zesty Fish with Fruit Salsa

Prep Time: 15 minutes • **Cook Time:** 8 minutes

1. Preheat broiler or grill. Combine mustard and honey. Stir *2 tablespoons* mustard mixture into fruit; set aside.

2. Brush remaining mustard mixture on both sides of fillets. Place in foil-lined broiler pan. Broil (or grill) fish 6 inches from heat for 8 minutes or until fish is opaque.

3. Serve fruit salsa with fish.

Makes 4 servings

Tip: To prepare this meal even faster, purchase cut-up fresh fruit from the salad bar.

¼ cup *French's* Spicy Brown Mustard
¼ cup honey
2 cups chopped assorted fresh fruit (pineapple, kiwi, strawberries and mango)
1 pound sea bass or cod fillets or other firm-fleshed white fish

Seafood Risotto

Prep Time: 5 minutes • **Cook Time:** 15 minutes

• In 4-quart saucepan, prepare rice according to package directions. Add frozen shrimp and vegetables during last 10 minutes of cooking time.

• Sprinkle with cheese.

Makes 4 servings

Serving Suggestion: Serve with garlic bread and a tossed green salad.

1 package (5.2 ounces) rice in creamy sauce (Risotto Milanese flavor)
1 package (14 to 16 ounces) frozen fully cooked shrimp
1 box (10 ounces) BIRDS EYE® frozen Mixed Vegetables
2 teaspoons grated Parmesan cheese

Italian Cheese Steaks

Prep Time: 5 minutes • **Cook Time:** 10 minutes

4 boneless sirloin steaks
   (6 to 8 ounces each)
1 tablespoon olive oil
1 jar (1 pound 10 ounces)
   RAGÚ® ROBUSTO!®
   Pasta Sauce
⅛ to ¼ teaspoon crushed
   red pepper flakes
   (optional)
1 cup shredded mozzarella
   cheese (about
   4 ounces)

1. Season steaks, if desired, with salt and ground black pepper.

2. In 12-inch skillet, heat olive oil over medium-high heat and brown steaks, turning occasionally, 4 minutes or until steaks are almost done. Remove steaks and set aside.

3. In same skillet, stir in Pasta Sauce and red pepper flakes. Cook, stirring frequently, 2 minutes. Return steaks to skillet; top steaks with cheese. Cook, covered, over medium heat 2 minutes or until cheese is melted. To serve, arrange steaks on platter. Pour Pasta Sauce around steaks and garnish, if desired, with chopped fresh parsley.

Makes 4 servings

Swiss Burgers

1½ pounds ground beef
¾ cup shredded Swiss
   cheese (about
   3 ounces)
1 can (8 ounces)
   sauerkraut, heated and
   drained
⅓ cup WISH-BONE®
   Thousand Island or Just
   2 Good! Thousand
   Island Dressing

Shape ground beef into 6 patties. Grill or broil until desired doneness. Top evenly with cheese, sauerkraut and Thousand Island dressing. Serve, if desired, with rye or pita bread.

Makes about 6 servings

helpful hint:

Ground beef is a fairly meaningless term. Most people want to know what kind of beef has been ground. To meet USDA standards, all ground beef must be at least 70 percent lean. The leanest are ground sirloin and ground round. Ground chuck contains more fat and therefore produces juicier hamburgers and meat loaf.

Hearty Stuffed Peppers

Prep Time: 15 minutes • **Cook Time:** 55 minutes

4 large green bell peppers,
    cored and seeded
1 jar (2 pounds) RAGÚ®
    Rich & Meaty Meat
    Sauce
1 cup shredded mozzarella
    cheese (about
    4 ounces)
1 cup uncooked instant rice
1 cup water

1. Preheat oven to 375°F. In 9-inch baking dish, arrange peppers; set aside.

2. In large bowl, combine Meat Sauce, ½ cup cheese and uncooked rice. Evenly stuff peppers with sauce mixture. Pour water in dish then cover with aluminum foil. Bake 50 minutes or until peppers are tender. Remove foil and top with remaining ½ cup cheese. Bake 5 minutes or until cheese is melted.

Makes 4 servings

Mustard Glazed Pork Loin

Prep Time: 10 minutes • **Cook Time:** 90 to 120 minutes

1 cup KARO® Light or Dark
    Corn Syrup
⅓ cup brown sugar
¼ cup mustard
1 (3- to 4-pound) pork loin

1. Preheat oven to 350°F. In a small bowl combine corn syrup, brown sugar and mustard.

2. Place pork in small roasting pan. Bake for 1½ to 2 hours (30 minutes per pound), or to desired doneness.

3. Brush with glaze several times during last 30 minutes of cooking.

Makes 4 to 6 servings

Variation: Add ½ teaspoon of rosemary or sage for added flavor.

Grilled Sherry Pork Chops

¼ cup HOLLAND HOUSE®
  Sherry Cooking Wine
¼ cup GRANDMA'S®
  Molasses
2 tablespoons soy sauce
4 pork chops (1 inch thick)

In plastic bowl, combine sherry, molasses and soy sauce; pour over pork chops. Cover; refrigerate 30 minutes. Prepare grill. Drain pork chops, reserving marinade. Grill pork chops over medium-high heat 20 to 30 minutes or until pork is no longer pink in center, turning once and brushing frequently with reserved marinade.* Discard any remaining marinade.   *Makes 4 servings*

*Do not baste during last 5 minutes of grilling.

Marinated Flank Steak with Pineapple

Prep and Marinate Time: 35 minutes • **Cook Time:** 8 to 12 minutes

1 can (15¼ ounces) DEL
  MONTE® Sliced
  Pineapple In Its Own
  Juice
¼ cup teriyaki sauce
2 tablespoons honey
1 pound beef flank steak

1. Drain pineapple, reserving 2 tablespoons juice. Set aside pineapple for later use.

2. Combine reserved juice, teriyaki sauce and honey in shallow 2-quart dish; mix well. Add meat; turn to coat. Cover; refrigerate at least 30 minutes or overnight.

3. Remove meat from marinade, reserving marinade. Grill meat over hot coals (or broil), brushing occasionally with reserved marinade. (Do not baste during last 5 minutes of cooking.) Cook about 4 minutes on each side for rare; about 5 minutes on each side for medium; or about 6 minutes on each side for well done. During last 4 minutes of cooking, grill pineapple until heated through.

4. Slice meat across grain; serve with pineapple. Garnish, if desired.   *Makes 4 servings*

Note: Marinade that has come into contact with raw meat must be discarded or boiled for several minutes before serving with cooked food.

Roasted Chicken au Jus

1 envelope LIPTON®
   RECIPE SECRETS®
   Onion Soup Mix*
2 tablespoons BERTOLLI®
   Olive Oil
1 (2½- to 3-pound)
   chicken, cut into
   serving pieces
½ cup hot water

*Also terrific with LIPTON®
RECIPE SECRETS® Savory
Herb with Garlic or Onion
Mushroom Soup Mix.*

1. Preheat oven to 425°F. In large bowl, combine soup mix and oil; add chicken and toss until evenly coated.

2. In bottom of broiler pan without rack, arrange chicken. Roast chicken, basting occasionally, 40 minutes or until chicken is thoroughly cooked.

3. Remove chicken to serving platter. Add hot water to pan and stir, scraping brown bits from bottom of pan. Serve sauce over chicken.
Makes 4 servings

Slow Cooker Method: Rub chicken pieces with soup mix combined with oil. Place chicken in slow cooker. Cover. Cook on HIGH 4 hours or LOW 6 to 8 hours. Serve as above.

Grilled Salmon Fillets

Prep Time: 10 minutes • **Cook Time:** 10 minutes

1 tablespoon MRS. DASH®
   Lemon Pepper
   seasoning
2 tablespoons whole grain
   Dijon mustard
3 tablespoons olive oil
6 (6-ounce) salmon fillets

Mix Mrs. Dash® Lemon Pepper seasoning, whole grain Dijon mustard and olive oil in small bowl. Rub mixture into salmon fillets. Place salmon in glass dish and refrigerate for 1 hour. Preheat grill to medium high. Place fillets skin side down and cook 5 to 6 minutes; turn carefully and continue cooking another 5 to 6 minutes. Serve immediately.
Makes 6 servings

Italian Beef

1 beef rump roast (3 to
    5 pounds)
1 can (14 ounces) beef
    broth
2 cups mixed vegetables
    such as celery, bell
    peppers, onion and/or
    carrots
8 Italian bread rolls

SLOW COOKER DIRECTIONS

1. Place rump roast in slow cooker; add beef broth and vegetables.

2. Cover; cook on LOW 10 hours.

3. Shred beef; serve with sauce on crusty Italian rolls.

Makes 8 servings

Polska Kielbasa Simmered in Beer and Onions

4 tablespoons butter
4 onions, thinly sliced
1 pound HILLSHIRE FARM®
    Polska Kielbasa,
    diagonally sliced into
    ¼-inch pieces
1 bottle (12 ounces) beer

Melt butter in large skillet over medium heat; sauté onions 4 to 5 minutes. Add Polska Kielbasa; brown 3 to 4 minutes on each side. Pour beer into skillet; bring to a boil. Reduce heat and simmer, uncovered, 25 minutes.

Makes 4 to 6 servings

Ragú® Fettuccine Carbonara

Prep Time: 5 minutes • **Cook Time:** 20 minutes

1 box (12 ounces)
    fettuccine
1 cup frozen green peas
1 jar (1 pound) RAGÚ®
    Cheesy! Classic Alfredo
    Sauce
4 slices bacon, crisp-
    cooked and crumbled

1. Cook fettuccine according to package directions, adding peas during last 2 minutes of cooking; drain and set aside.

2. In 2-quart saucepan, heat Alfredo Sauce; stir in bacon.

3. To serve, toss Alfredo Sauce with hot fettuccine and peas. Sprinkle, if desired, with ground black pepper and grated Parmesan cheese.

Makes 6 servings

Parmesan Crusted Chicken

Prep Time: 10 minutes • **Cook Time:** 20 minutes

½ cup HELLMANN'S® or
    BEST FOODS® Real
    Mayonnaise
¼ cup grated Parmesan
    cheese
4 boneless, skinless chicken
    breast halves (about
    1¼ pounds)
4 teaspoons Italian
    seasoned dry bread
    crumbs

1. Preheat oven to 425°F.

2. In medium bowl, combine Hellmann's or Best Foods Real Mayonnaise and cheese. On baking sheet, arrange chicken. Evenly top with mayonnaise mixture, then sprinkle with bread crumbs.

3. Bake 20 minutes or until chicken is thoroughly cooked.

Makes 4 servings

4
ingredients

Harvest Ham Supper

6 carrots, cut into 2-inch pieces
3 medium sweet potatoes, quartered
1 to 1½ pounds boneless ham
1 cup maple syrup

SLOW COOKER DIRECTIONS

1. Place carrots and potatoes in bottom of slow cooker. Place ham on top of vegetables. Pour syrup over ham and vegetables.

2. Cover; cook on LOW 6 to 8 hours.

Makes 6 servings

Cheesy Turkey Veg•All® Bake

Prep Time: 7 minutes • **Cook Time:** 20 minutes

1 package (5½ ounces) au gratin potato mix
2⅔ cups boiling water
1 can (15 ounces) VEG•ALL® Original Mixed Vegetables, drained
1 cup cubed cooked turkey
2 tablespoons butter

Preheat oven to 350°F. Place au gratin potato mix and sauce packet into large mixing bowl. Add water, Veg•All, turkey and butter; mix well. Pour into ungreased 2-quart casserole. Bake for 20 minutes or until top is golden brown. Cool for 5 minutes before serving.

Makes 6 servings

4 Sweet Temptations

ingredients

2 packages (18 ounces each) refrigerated chocolate chip cookie dough
2 packages (8 ounces each) cream cheese, softened
½ cup sugar
2 eggs

Cheesecake Cookie Bars

1. Preheat oven to 350°F. Lightly grease 13×9-inch baking pan. Let both doughs stand at room temperature about 15 minutes.

2. Reserve ¾ of one package of dough. Press remaining 1¼ packages of dough evenly onto bottom of prepared pan.

3. Combine cream cheese, sugar and eggs in large bowl; beat until well blended and smooth. Spread cream cheese mixture over dough in pan. Break reserved dough into small pieces; sprinkle over cream cheese mixture.

4. Bake 35 minutes or until center is almost set. Cool completely in pan on wire rack. Store leftovers covered in refrigerator.

Makes about 2 dozen bars

Vanilla Ice Cream Loaf

¼ cup powdered sugar
1 package (3 ounces) ladyfingers, separated
1½ quarts vanilla ice cream, softened
1 cup raspberry or strawberry sauce
Fresh or thawed frozen raspberries or strawberries (optional)

1. Line 9×5-inch loaf pan with plastic wrap, leaving 2½-inch overhang on all sides.

2. Combine powdered sugar and 1 to 2 teaspoons water in small bowl; stir until well blended and pasty. Spread small amount of powdered sugar mixture on bottom of 1 ladyfinger; anchor it upright against side of pan. Repeat with remaining ladyfingers, making border around pan.

3. Beat ice cream in large bowl with electric mixer until smooth. Spread in pan, pressing against ladyfingers. Cover and freeze 6 hours or overnight.

4. Place loaf in refrigerator 20 minutes before serving. Carefully remove ice cream loaf from pan using plastic overhang. To serve, drizzle 1 tablespoon sauce onto individual serving plates. Cut loaf into slices; place over sauce. Drizzle another 1 tablespoon sauce over top. Top with raspberries, if desired.   *Makes 8 servings*

Watermelon Dippers

8 ounces sour cream
¼ cup sugar
1 teaspoon vanilla extract
Watermelon sticks or small wedges

Combine the sour cream, sugar and vanilla in a small serving bowl; stir until well blended. Use as a dip for the watermelon.
Makes about 8 servings

Favorite recipe from *National Watermelon Promotion Board*

Festive Fudge

3 cups (18 ounces)
    semisweet or milk
    chocolate chips
1 (14-ounce) can EAGLE
    BRAND® Sweetened
    Condensed Milk
    (NOT evaporated milk)
    Dash salt
½ to 1 cup chopped nuts
1½ teaspoons vanilla extract

1. In heavy saucepan, over low heat, melt chocolate chips with EAGLE BRAND® and salt. Remove from heat; stir in nuts and vanilla. Spread evenly into wax paper lined 8- or 9-inch square pan. Chill 2 hours or until firm.

2. Turn fudge onto cutting board; peel off paper and cut into squares. Store leftovers covered in refrigerator.

Makes about 2 pounds

Chocolate Peanut Butter Chip Glazed Fudge: Substitute ¾ cup peanut butter chips for nuts. For glaze, melt additional ½ cup peanut butter chips with ½ cup whipping cream; stir until thick and smooth. Spread over fudge.

Marshmallow Fudge: Add 2 tablespoons butter to chocolate mixture. Substitute 2 cups miniature marshmallows for nuts.

Gift Tips: Create delicious homemade gifts from an assortment of flavored fudges, packed in decorative tins, candy bags or boxes. Wrap individual pieces of fudge in colored food-grade cellophane, candy wrappers or gold or silver foil candy cups and arrange in gift bags or tins. Store in refrigerator.

Paradise Freeze

Prep Time: 10 minutes

1 large ripe DOLE® Banana
1 cup DOLE® Strawberries
1 ripe DOLE® Mango,
    cubed
1 cup cranberry juice
1 cup ice cubes

• Combine banana, strawberries, mango, juice and ice in blender or food processor container. Cover; blend until thick and smooth.

Makes 3 servings

White & Chocolate Covered Strawberries

2 cups (12-ounce package) HERSHEY'S Premier White Chips
2 tablespoons shortening (do not use butter, margarine, spread or oil), divided
1 cup HERSHEY'S Semi-Sweet Chocolate Chips
4 cups (2 pints) fresh strawberries, rinsed, patted dry and chilled

1. Cover tray with wax paper.

2. Place white chips and 1 tablespoon shortening in medium microwave-safe bowl. Microwave at HIGH (100%) 1 minute; stir until chips are melted and mixture is smooth. If necessary, microwave at HIGH an additional 30 seconds at a time, just until smooth when stirred.

3. Holding by top, dip ⅔ of each strawberry into white chip mixture; shake gently to remove excess. Place on prepared tray; refrigerate until coating is firm, at least 30 minutes.

4. Repeat microwave procedure with chocolate chips and remaining shortening in clean microwave-safe bowl. Dip lower ⅓ of each berry into chocolate mixture. Refrigerate until firm. Cover; refrigerate leftover strawberries. *Makes 2 to 3 dozen berries*

Lemon Icebox Pie

1 (14-ounce) can EAGLE BRAND® Sweetened Condensed Milk (NOT evaporated milk)
½ cup lemon juice
Yellow food coloring (optional)
1 cup (½ pint) whipping cream, whipped
1 (6-ounce) prepared graham cracker or baked pie crust

1. In medium bowl, combine EAGLE BRAND®, lemon juice and food coloring (optional). Fold in whipped cream.

2. Pour into prepared crust. Chill 3 hours or until set. Garnish as desired. Store leftovers covered in refrigerator.

Makes one 9-inch pie

4 ingredients

Brown Sugar Shortbread

1 cup I CAN'T BELIEVE IT'S NOT BUTTER!® Spread
¾ cup firmly packed light brown sugar
2 cups all-purpose flour
⅓ cup semisweet chocolate chips, melted

Preheat oven to 325°F. Grease 9-inch round cake pan; set aside.

In large bowl, with electric mixer, beat I Can't Believe It's Not Butter!® Spread and brown sugar until light and fluffy, about 5 minutes. Gradually add flour and beat on low until blended. Spread mixture into prepared pan and press into even layer. With knife, score surface into 16 pie-shaped wedges.

Bake 45 minutes or until lightly golden. On wire rack, cool 20 minutes; remove from pan and cool completely. Cut into wedges. To decorate, place melted chocolate in small food storage bag. Snip off corner of bag; drizzle chocolate over shortbread.

Makes 16 servings

Speedy Pineapple-Lime Sorbet

1 ripe pineapple, cut into cubes (about 4 cups)
⅓ cup frozen limeade concentrate, thawed
1 to 2 tablespoons fresh lime juice
1 teaspoon freshly grated lime peel

1. Arrange pineapple in single layer on large baking sheet; freeze at least 1 hour or until very firm.*

2. Combine frozen pineapple, limeade, lime juice and lime peel in food processor; cover and process until smooth and fluffy. If mixture doesn't become smooth and fluffy, let stand 30 minutes to soften slightly; repeat processing. Serve immediately.

Makes 8 servings

Pineapple can be frozen up to 1 month in resealable freezer food storage bags.

Note: This dessert is best if served immediately, but it can be made ahead, stored in the freezer and then softened several minutes before being served.

Peach Parfait Pie

Prep Time: 10 minutes • **Freeze Time:** 3 hours

½ cup boiling water
1 (3-ounce) package peach flavored gelatin
1 pint vanilla ice cream, softened
2 cups sliced fresh peaches
1 (6-ounce) READY CRUST® Shortbread Pie Crust

1. Pour boiling water over peach gelatin in medium bowl; stir until gelatin dissolves.

2. Add ice cream; stir until smooth. Fold in peaches. Pour into crust.

3. Freeze until set, about 3 hours. Freeze leftovers.

Makes 8 servings

Skippy Quick Cookies

Prep Time: 10 minutes • **Cook Time:** 8 minutes

1 cup SKIPPY® Creamy or Super Chunk® Peanut Butter
1 cup sugar
1 egg, slightly beaten
1 teaspoon vanilla extract

Preheat oven to 325°F. In medium bowl, combine all ingredients. Shape dough into 1-inch balls. On ungreased baking sheets, arrange cookies 2 inches apart. With fork, gently flatten each cookie and press crisscross pattern into top.

Bake 8 minutes or until lightly browned and slightly puffed. Immediately top, if desired, with sprinkles, chocolate chips or chocolate candies. On wire rack, cool completely before removing from baking sheets. *Makes 2 dozen cookies*

Note: This simple recipe is unusual because it doesn't contain any flour—but it still makes great cookies!

Coconut Custard

Prep Time: 15 minutes • **Chill Time:** 40 minutes

1. In a medium saucepan, stir 1 cup of the coconut milk into the corn starch until dissolved.

2. Add remaining coconut milk, the Karo and the salt. Cook over medium high heat until boiling, stirring constantly until it thickens.

3. Pour into individual serving dishes. Sprinkle with cinnamon and refrigerate to chill.

Makes 10 servings

2 cups KARO® Light Corn
   Syrup
4 cups coconut milk
²/₃ cup ARGO® Corn Starch
¼ teaspoon salt
   Ground cinnamon

Ho Ho® Pudding

Cut Ho Ho's into circles, saving 1 Ho Ho. Mix pudding and milk according to package pudding directions and chill until thick. In large glass bowl, layer Ho Ho's, pudding and whipped topping. Ending with whipped topping. Take remaining Ho Ho and slice in circles and place on top. Keep refrigerated until ready to eat.

Makes 10 to 12 servings

Tip: For a Halloween treat, tint the whipped topping orange to create an orange and black dessert.

1 box (10 ounces) of
   HO HO'S®
2 packages (4-serving size
   each) instant chocolate
   pudding mix
4 cups milk
1 large tub (16 ounces)
   whipped topping

4
ingredients

Ricotta Cheese and Blueberry Parfait

1 cup whole milk ricotta
   cheese
1 tablespoon powdered
   sugar
   Grated peel of 1 lemon
1½ cups fresh blueberries

1. Combine ricotta cheese, sugar and lemon peel in medium bowl; mix well.

2. Place 3 tablespoons blueberries in each of 4 parfait glasses. Add ¼ cup ricotta cheese mixture; top with another 3 tablespoons blueberries. Garnish as desired.

Makes 4 servings

Chocolate Satin Pie

1 *prepared* 9-inch
   (6 ounces) graham
   cracker crumb crust
1 can (12 fluid ounces)
   NESTLÉ® CARNATION®
   Evaporated Milk
2 large egg yolks
2 cups (12-ounce package)
   NESTLÉ® TOLL HOUSE®
   Semi-Sweet Chocolate
   Morsels
   Whipped cream
   (optional)
   Chopped nuts (optional)

WHISK together evaporated milk and egg yolks in medium saucepan. Heat over medium-low heat, stirring constantly, until mixture is very hot and thickens slightly; do not boil. Remove from heat; stir in morsels until completely melted and mixture is smooth.

POUR into crust; refrigerate for 3 hours or until firm. Top with whipped cream before serving; sprinkle with nuts.

Makes 10 servings

Hershey's Premier White Chips Almond Fudge

2 cups (12-ounce package) HERSHEY'S Premier White Chips
²/₃ cup sweetened condensed milk (not evaporated milk)
1½ cups coarsely chopped slivered almonds, toasted*
½ teaspoon vanilla extract

*To toast almonds: Spread almonds in even layer on cookie sheet. Bake at 350°F 8 to 10 minutes or until lightly browned, stirring occasionally; cool.

1. Line 8-inch square pan with foil, extending foil over edges of pan.

2. Melt white chips with sweetened condensed milk in medium saucepan over very low heat, stirring constantly until mixture is smooth. Remove from heat. Stir in almonds and vanilla. Spread into prepared pan.

3. Cover; refrigerate 2 hours or until firm. Use foil to lift fudge out of pan; peel off foil. Cut fudge into squares.

Makes about 3 dozen pieces or 1½ pounds fudge

Note: For best results, do not double this recipe.

Honey Strawberry Tart

⅓ cup honey
1 tablespoon lemon juice
1 baked or ready-to-eat 9-inch pie shell
4 cups halved fresh strawberries
Mint sprigs for garnish (optional)

Combine honey and lemon juice in small bowl; mix well. Brush bottom of pie shell with mixture. Fill shell with strawberries. Drizzle remaining honey mixture over berries. Garnish with mint sprigs, if desired.

Makes 8 servings

Tip: Prepare honey glaze and strawberries. Fill shell and glaze strawberries just before serving to prevent shell from becoming soggy.

Favorite recipe from **National Honey Board**

HERSHEY'S® PREMIER WHITE CHIPS ALMOND FUDGE

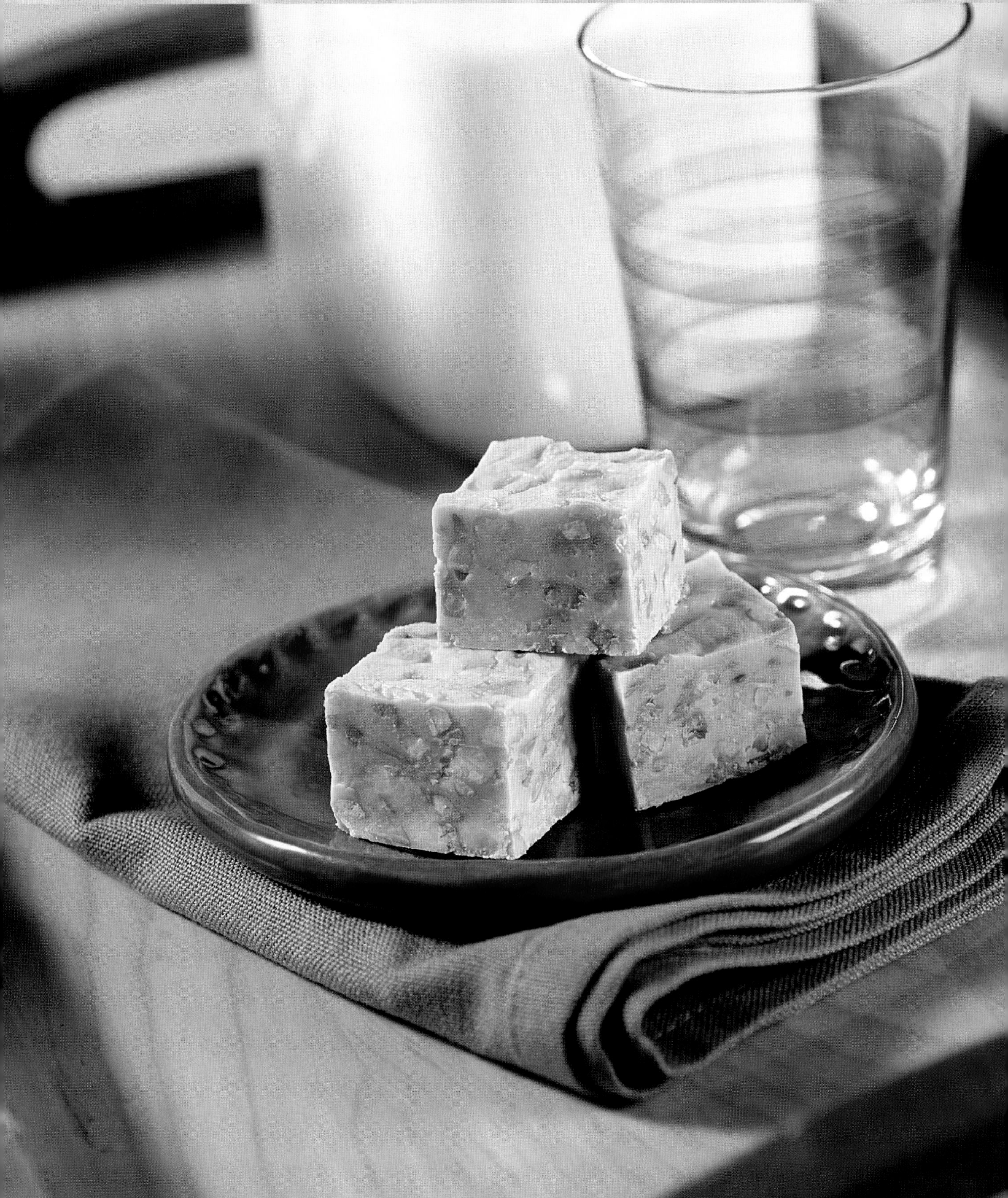

4 ingredients

Bananas Foster

Prep Time: 5 minutes • **Cook Time:** 5 minutes

6 tablespoons I CAN'T
  BELIEVE IT'S NOT
  BUTTER!® Spread
3 tablespoons firmly
  packed brown sugar
4 ripe medium bananas,
  sliced diagonally
2 tablespoons dark rum or
  brandy (optional)
  Vanilla ice cream

In 12-inch skillet, bring I Can't Believe It's Not Butter!® Spread, brown sugar and bananas to a boil. Cook 2 minutes, stirring gently. Carefully add rum to center of pan and cook 15 seconds. Serve hot banana mixture over scoops of ice cream and top, if desired, with sweetened whipped cream. *Makes 4 servings*

Note: Choose ripe but firm bananas for this recipe. They will hold their shape better when cooked.

Irresistible Peach Smoothies

2 cups peeled, pitted and
  diced fresh Washington
  peaches
½ cup lowfat milk
1 cup vanilla ice cream
1 tablespoon fresh lemon
  juice

Combine all ingredients in blender container and blend until smooth. *Makes 3 servings*

Tip: For a super cold smoothie, layer diced peaches in a single layer on a freezer-safe pan and freeze 1 hour or until completely frozen.

Favorite recipe from *Washington State Fruit Commission*

4 ingredients

Fluted Kisses® Cups with Peanut Butter Filling

72 HERSHEY'S KISSES®
    Brand Milk Chocolates,
    divided
1 cup REESE'S® Creamy
    Peanut Butter
1 cup powdered sugar
1 tablespoon butter or
    margarine, softened

1. Line small baking cups (1¾ inches in diameter) with small paper bake cups. Remove wrappers from chocolates.

2. Place 48 chocolates in small microwave-safe bowl. Microwave at HIGH (100%) 1 minute or until chocolate is melted and smooth when stirred. Using small brush, coat inside of paper cups with melted chocolate.

3. Refrigerate 20 minutes; reapply melted chocolate to any thin spots. Refrigerate until firm, preferably overnight. Gently peel paper from chocolate cups.

4. Beat peanut butter, powdered sugar and butter with electric mixer on medium speed in small bowl until smooth. Spoon into chocolate cups. Before serving, top each cup with a chocolate piece. Cover; store cups in refrigerator.

Makes about 2 dozen pieces

helpful hint:

When melting chocolate, make sure that all utensils are completely dry. Moisture, whether from utensils or a drop of water, may cause chocolate to become stiff and grainy. If this happens, try adding ½ teaspoon of shortening (not butter or margarine, which contain water) for each ounce of chocolate and stir until smooth.

5

ingredients..

5 Table of Contents
ingredients

5 Awesome Appetizers
ingredients

Roasted Red Potato Bites

Prep Time: 10 minutes • **Cook Time:** 40 minutes

1½ pounds red potatoes
(about 15 small)
1 cup shredded cheddar
cheese (about
4 ounces)
½ cup HELLMANN'S® or
BEST FOODS® Real
Mayonnaise
½ cup sliced green onions
2 tablespoons chopped
fresh basil leaves
(optional)
10 slices bacon, crisp-
cooked and crumbled

1. Preheat oven to 400°F. On large baking sheet, arrange potatoes and bake 35 minutes or until tender. Let stand until cool enough to handle.

2. Cut each potato in half, then cut thin slice from bottom of each potato half. With small melon baller or spoon, scoop pulp from potatoes leaving ¼-inch shell. Place pulp in medium bowl; set shells aside.

3. In medium bowl, lightly mash pulp. Stir in remaining ingredients. Spoon or pipe potato filling into potato shells.

4. Arrange filled shells on baking sheet and broil 3 minutes or until golden and heated through.   *Makes 30 bites*

Olive Tapenade Dip

Prep Time: 10 minutes

1½ cups (10-ounce jar) pitted kalamata olives
3 tablespoons olive oil
3 tablespoons *French's®* Spicy Brown Mustard
1 tablespoon minced fresh rosemary leaves *or* 1 teaspoon dried rosemary leaves
1 teaspoon minced garlic

1. Place all ingredients in food processor. Process until puréed.

2. Serve with vegetable crudités or pita chips.

Makes 4 (¼-cup) servings

Tip: To easily pit the olives, first place them in a plastic bag. Then gently tap them with a wooden mallet or rolling pin until the olives split open. Remove and discard the pits.

Sensational Stuffed Mushrooms

30 large mushrooms (about 1 pound)
½ pound bulk pork sausage
1 cup chopped dried tart cherries
1 (8-ounce) package cream cheese, softened
2 green onions, sliced

Preheat oven to 425°F. Pull stems from mushrooms and discard (or save for another use). Rinse mushroom caps; drain well. Set aside.

Cook sausage in large skillet, stirring to break up meat, 5 minutes or until sausage is done. Remove from heat. Add dried cherries, cream cheese and onions; mix well. Fill each mushroom cap with heaping teaspoonful of sausage mixture.

Place filled mushrooms on lightly greased baking sheet. Bake for 6 to 8 minutes. Serve immediately. *Makes 30 appetizers*

Favorite recipe from **Cherry Marketing Institute**

Tortilla Crunch Chicken Fingers

1 envelope LIPTON®
  RECIPE SECRETS®
  Savory Herb with
  Garlic Soup Mix
1 cup finely crushed plain
  tortilla chips or
  cornflakes (about
  3 ounces)
1½ pounds boneless, skinless
  chicken breasts, cut
  into strips
1 egg
2 tablespoons water
2 tablespoons I CAN'T
  BELIEVE IT'S NOT
  BUTTER!® Spread,
  melted

1. Preheat oven to 400°F.

2. In medium bowl, combine soup mix and tortilla chips. In large plastic bag or large bowl, combine chicken and egg beaten with water until evenly coated. Remove chicken and dip in tortilla mixture until evenly coated; discard bag. On 15½×10½×1-inch jelly-roll pan sprayed with nonstick cooking spray, arrange chicken; drizzle with I Can't Believe It's Not Butter!® Spread. Bake, uncovered, 12 minutes or until chicken is thoroughly cooked. Serve with chunky salsa, if desired.

Makes about 24 chicken fingers

Roast Beef Crostini with Spicy Horseradish Sauce

1 baguette French bread
½ cup mayonnaise
4 tablespoons prepared
  horseradish, drained
1 teaspoon TABASCO®
  brand Pepper Sauce
8 ounces roast beef, cooked
  medium rare, thinly
  sliced*
  Freshly ground black
  pepper

Deli sliced roast beef can be substituted.

Slice baguette into rounds ½ inch thick. Toast bread in toaster oven or broiler until light brown on both sides. Set aside.

Blend mayonnaise, horseradish and TABASCO® Sauce in small bowl. Spread generously on toast rounds. Top with roast beef slices; sprinkle with pepper. *Makes about 30 crostini*

helpful hint:

Horseradish is a large, white root with a pungent flavor. It can be found fresh occasionally in produce markets, but it is most commonly found grated, preserved in vinegar and packed in jars in the refrigerated section of the supermarket. It is referred to as prepared horseradish in recipes. Once opened it loses its pungency quickly so plan to use it within a few weeks.

Vermont Fiesta Paulkets

2 (10-ounce) packages refrigerated pizza dough
½ pound deli-style mesquite turkey breast, shaved
8 ounces Vermont mild Cheddar cheese, shredded
1 (11-ounce) jar NEWMAN'S OWN® Medium Salsa
1 (8-ounce) container sour cream

Preheat oven to 425°F. On floured board, unroll both packages of pizza dough and cut each into 4 squares, about 5 inches each.

Evenly arrange turkey breast, cheese and salsa (about 2 tablespoons each) diagonally on half of each dough square. Fold empty side down over filling. Turn bottom edge over top edge and pinch to seal.

Place Paulkets on *ungreased* cookie sheet and bake about 20 minutes or until dough is cooked through and lightly browned. (If sealed improperly they may leak, but will still taste delicious.)

Serve with generous amounts of Newman's Own® Medium Salsa and sour cream.

Makes 8 Paulkets

Hidden Valley® Bacon-Cheddar Ranch Dip

1 container (16 ounces) sour cream (2 cups)
1 packet (1 ounce) HIDDEN VALLEY® The Original Ranch® Dips Mix
1 cup (4 ounces) shredded Cheddar cheese
¼ cup crisp-cooked, crumbled bacon*
Potato chips or corn chips, for dipping

Bacon pieces can be used.

Combine sour cream and dips mix in a medium bowl. Stir in cheese and bacon. Chill at least 1 hour. Garnish as desired. Serve with chips.

Makes about 3 cups dip

Pastry Puffs with Goat Cheese and Spinach

1 (12-ounce) package BOB EVANS® Original Links
30 to 40 leaves fresh spinach
1 (17¾-ounce) package frozen puff pastry sheets, thawed according to package directions
⅓ cup goat cheese*
3 tablespoons Dijon mustard

For a milder flavor, substitute plain or herb cream cheese for goat cheese.

Cook sausage in large skillet until browned. Drain on paper towels; let cool. Steam spinach; let cool. Preheat oven to 375°F. Cut 1 pastry sheet evenly into 9 squares. Cut 5 additional squares from second sheet (remaining pastry may be refrozen for future use). Stretch or roll squares slightly to form rectangles. Line each rectangle with 2 or 3 spinach leaves, leaving ¼ inch on 1 short end to seal edges. Spread about 1 teaspoon goat cheese over spinach; spread ½ teaspoon mustard over goat cheese. Arrange sausage across short end and roll up pastry and filling, pressing to seal edges. Place on *ungreased* baking sheet, seam sides down. Bake 14 to 16 minutes or until golden. Cut each puff into halves or thirds. Refrigerate leftovers.   *Makes 28 to 42 appetizers*

Note: Pastry puffs may be made ahead and refrigerated overnight or frozen up to 1 month. Reheat in oven when ready to serve.

Lava Pizza Dip

Prep Time: 5 minutes • **Cook Time:** 10 minutes

1 cup RAGÚ® OLD WORLD STYLE® Pasta Sauce
1 cup RAGÚ® Cheesy! Classic Alfredo Sauce
1 cup shredded mozzarella cheese (about 4 ounces)
¼ cup finely chopped pepperoni
½ cup diced red or orange bell pepper

1. In 2-quart saucepan, heat all ingredients, stirring occasionally, 10 minutes or until cheese is melted.

2. Transfer to 1½-quart casserole or serving bowl and serve, if desired, with cooked meatballs, Italian bread cubes, baby carrots, broccoli florets or cherry tomatoes for dipping.   *Makes 2 cups dip*

Mini SPAM® Classic & Cheese Buns

1 (1-pound) loaf frozen bread dough, thawed
1 (12-ounce) can SPAM® Classic, shredded
1½ cups (6 ounces) shredded Monterey Jack cheese
2 teaspoons dried dill weed
1 egg
1 tablespoon water

Cut bread dough in half lengthwise; cut each half into 12 pieces. In medium bowl, combine SPAM®, cheese and dill weed; mix well. Place about 1 tablespoon SPAM™ mixture in center of 1 piece of dough. Shape dough into a ball; place on greased baking sheet. Repeat with remaining dough pieces. Cover; let rise in warm place 30 to 40 minutes or until doubled in bulk. Heat oven to 350°F. Uncover dough. In small bowl, stir together egg and water. Brush each piece of dough with egg mixture. Bake 20 to 30 minutes or until golden brown. Serve warm.*   *Makes 24 appetizers*

*To reheat buns, wrap in aluminum foil. Bake 10 to 15 minutes or until thoroughly heated. Buns can be frozen. Seal in freezer-weight plastic food storage bags and freeze up to 2 months. Reheat as directed.

Saucy Mini Franks

Prep Time: 5 minutes • **Cook Time:** 5 minutes

½ cup *French's®* Honey Mustard
½ cup chili sauce or ketchup
½ cup grape jelly
1 tablespoon *Frank's® RedHot®* Original Cayenne Pepper Sauce
1 pound mini cocktail franks or 1 pound cooked meatballs

1. Combine mustard, chili sauce, grape jelly and *Frank's RedHot* Sauce in saucepan.

2. Add cocktail franks. Simmer and stir 5 minutes or until jelly is melted and franks are hot.   *Makes about 6 servings*

Braunschweiger Dip

1 cup mayonnaise
1 cup (½ pint) sour cream
1 packet (1 ounce)
    HIDDEN VALLEY® The
    Original Ranch® Salad
    Dressing & Seasoning
    Mix
½ cup mashed
    braunschweiger (liver
    sausage)
3 tablespoons chopped
    green onions

Combine mayonnaise, sour cream and salad dressing & seasoning mix in a medium bowl. Stir in braunschweiger and green onions. Refrigerate at least 1 hour before serving. Serve with assorted breads and crackers.

Makes about 2½ cups dip

Chipotle Chili Hummus Dip

Prep Time: 5 minutes

½ cup *French's®*
    Gourmayo™ Smoked
    Chipotle Light
    Mayonnaise
½ cup prepared hummus dip
1 tablespoon *Frank's®*
    RedHot® Chile 'n
    Lime™ Hot Sauce or
    Frank's® RedHot®
    Cayenne Pepper Sauce
1 tablespoon minced green
    onion
½ teaspoon finely minced
    garlic

1. Combine all ingredients in small bowl until blended. Chill.

2. Serve with cut-up vegetables or chips.

Makes about 4 (¼-cup) servings

Tip: Use as a spread on sandwiches or wraps.

Hidden Valley® Torta

2 packages (8 ounces each) cream cheese, softened
1 packet (1 ounce) HIDDEN VALLEY® The Original Ranch® Salad Dressing & Seasoning Mix
1 jar (6 ounces) marinated artichoke hearts, drained and chopped
⅓ cup roasted red peppers, drained and chopped
3 tablespoons minced fresh parsley

Combine cream cheese and salad dressing & seasoning mix in a medium bowl. In a separate bowl, stir together artichokes, peppers and parsley. In a 3-cup bowl lined with plastic wrap, alternate layers of cream cheese mixture and vegetable mixture, beginning and ending with a cheese layer.

Chill 4 hours or overnight. Invert onto plate; remove plastic wrap. Serve with crackers.

Makes 10 to 12 servings

Bourbon Dogs

2 cups ketchup
¾ cup bourbon
½ cup dark brown sugar
1 tablespoon grated onion
1 pound HILLSHIRE FARM® Lit'l Smokies

Combine ketchup, bourbon, brown sugar and onion in medium saucepan. Stir in Lit'l Smokies; simmer in sauce over low heat or bake in 300°F oven 1 hour.* Serve hot.

Makes about 50 hors d'oeuvres

*If mixture becomes too thick, thin with additional bourbon or water.

SPAM™ Nachos

1 (10½-ounce) bag
   CHI-CHI'S® Tortilla
   Chips
1 (12-ounce) can SPAM®
   Classic, cubed
1 (16-ounce) jar
   CHI-CHI'S® Salsa
1 (16-ounce) can refried
   beans
1 (8-ounce) package
   shredded Mexican
   pasteurized processed
   cheese

Heat oven to 425°F. Place chips on baking sheet. Sprinkle SPAM® over chips. In medium bowl, combine CHI-CHI'S® Salsa and refried beans; pour over chips. Sprinkle with cheese. Bake 6 to 7 minutes or until cheese is melted. Serve immediately.

Makes 10 appetizer servings

Walnut Chicken Pinwheels

2 boneless skinless chicken
   breasts, cut into halves
12 to 14 spinach leaves
1 package (6.5 ounces)
   ALOUETTE® Garlic &
   Herbs Cheese
5 ounces roasted red
   peppers, sliced or
   5 ounces pimiento
   slices
¾ cup finely chopped
   California walnuts

Pound chicken to about ¼-inch thickness with flat side of meat mallet or chef's knife. Cover each chicken piece with spinach leaves. Spread each with Alouette. Top with pepper slices and walnuts. Carefully roll up each breast and secure with wooden toothpicks. Bake at 400°F 20 to 25 minutes or until cooked through. Chill. Just before serving, remove toothpicks and slice into ½-inch rounds. Serve cold.

Makes about 35 appetizers

5

ingredients

Chunky Hawaiian Spread

1 package (3 ounces) light
  cream cheese, softened
½ cup fat free or light sour
  cream
1 can (8 ounces) DOLE®
  Crushed Pineapple,
  well drained
¼ cup mango chutney*
  Low fat crackers

*If there are large pieces of
fruit in chutney, cut them into
smaller pieces.*

• Beat cream cheese, sour cream, crushed pineapple and chutney
in bowl until blended. Cover and chill 1 hour or overnight. Serve
with crackers. Refrigerate any leftover spread in airtight container
for up to one week.   *Makes 2½ cups spread*

Toasted Sun-Dried Tomato Bread

½ cup I CAN'T BELIEVE IT'S
  NOT BUTTER!® Spread
2 tablespoons finely
  chopped, drained
  sun-dried tomatoes
  packed in oil
1 shallot or small onion,
  finely chopped
1 clove garlic, finely
  chopped
1 loaf French or Italian
  bread (about 12 inches
  long), halved
  lengthwise

In small bowl, blend all ingredients except bread. Evenly spread
bread with sun-dried tomato mixture. On ungreased baking sheet,
arrange bread and broil until golden. Slice and serve.
                                          Makes about 12 servings

5 Side-Dish Sensations ingredients

Stir-Fried Asparagus

½ pound asparagus
1 tablespoon olive or
    canola oil
1 cup sliced celery
½ cup roasted red peppers,
    drained and diced
¼ cup sliced almonds,
    toasted*

*To toast almonds, place in
small dry skillet. Cook and
stir over medium heat until
lightly browned.

1. Trim and discard ends from asparagus. Slice stalks diagonally into 1-inch pieces.

2. Heat oil in 12-inch nonstick skillet over medium-high heat. Add celery; stir-fry 2 minutes. Add asparagus and red peppers; stir-fry 3 to 4 minutes or until asparagus is crisp-tender.

3. Add almonds and ¼ teaspoon black pepper; stir until blended.

Makes 6 servings

Swiss Onion Potatoes Rosti

Prep Time: 5 minutes • **Cook Time:** 15 minutes

1 tablespoon olive oil
½ cup crumbled cooked bacon
5 cups shredded fresh or frozen potatoes
1⅓ cups *French's®* French Fried Onions
1 cup (4 ounces) shredded Swiss or Cheddar cheese
Applesauce or sour cream (optional)

1. Heat oil in 10-inch nonstick skillet over medium-high heat. Cook bacon 1 minute. Stir in potatoes, French Fried Onions and cheese. Cook 8 minutes or until lightly browned on bottom.

2. Loosen mixture and gently invert onto large serving platter. Return to skillet and cook 6 minutes or until browned.

3. Remove to serving platter. Season to taste with salt and pepper. If desired, serve with dollop of applesauce or sour cream on the side.
Makes 4 to 6 servings

Honey Mustard Glazed Vegetables

Prep Time: 5 minutes • **Cook Time:** 7 minutes

2 tablespoons butter
1 package (10 ounces) frozen baby carrots, thawed
1½ cups frozen pearl onions
¼ cup *French's®* Honey Mustard
2 tablespoons sugar
1 tablespoon finely chopped fresh parsley (optional)

1. Melt butter in 12-inch nonstick skillet over medium-high heat. Sauté carrots and onions for 5 minutes until crisp-tender.

2. Stir in mustard and sugar. Cook, stirring occasionally, about 2 minutes until vegetables are glazed. Sprinkle with parsley, if desired.
Makes 4 servings

Apple-Rice Medley

1 package (6 ounces)
   long-grain and wild
   rice mix
1 cup (4 ounces) shredded
   mild Cheddar cheese,
   divided
1 cup chopped Washington
   Golden Delicious apple
1 cup sliced mushrooms
½ cup thinly sliced celery

Prepare rice mix according to package directions. Preheat oven to 350°F. Add ½ cup cheese, apple, mushrooms and celery to rice; toss to combine. Spoon mixture into 1-quart casserole dish. Bake 15 minutes. Top with remaining ½ cup cheese; bake until cheese melts, about 10 minutes.

Makes 4 servings

Microwave Directions: Combine cooked rice, ½ cup cheese, apple, mushrooms and celery as directed; spoon mixture into 1-quart microwave-safe dish. Microwave at HIGH 3 to 4 minutes or until heated through. Top with remaining ½ cup cheese; microwave at HIGH 1 minute or until cheese melts.

Favorite recipe from **Washington Apple Commission**

Vegetable Potato Salad

Prep Time: 20 minutes • **Chill Time:** 2 hours

1 envelope LIPTON®
   RECIPE SECRETS®
   Vegetable Soup Mix
1 cup HELLMANN'S® or
   BEST FOODS® Real
   Mayonnaise
2 teaspoons white vinegar
2 pounds red or all-purpose
   potatoes, cooked and
   cut into chunks
¼ cup finely chopped red
   onion

1. In large bowl, combine soup mix, mayonnaise and vinegar.

2. Add potatoes and onion; toss well. Chill 2 hours.

Makes 6 servings

5
ingredients

Cheesy Potato Gratin

Prep Time: 20 minutes • **Total Time:** 1 hour 20 minutes

3½ pounds baking potatoes,
   peeled and thinly sliced
2 tablespoons HERB-OX®
   chicken flavored
   bouillon, divided
3 cups shredded Havarti
   cheese, divided
6 tablespoons all-purpose
   flour, divided
3 cups heavy whipping
   cream

Heat oven to 400°F. Spray a 13×9-inch baking dish with nonstick cooking spray. Arrange one third of the potatoes in the baking dish. Sprinkle with 1 teaspoon bouillon and season to taste with freshly ground pepper. Add one third of the cheese and 2 tablespoons flour. Continue adding two more layers of potatoes, bouillon, pepper, flour and cheese. In bowl, combine whipping cream and remaining 1 tablespoon chicken bouillon. Pour mixture over the potatoes. Bake for 60 minutes or until the top is golden brown and the potatoes are tender.   *Makes 10 to 12 servings*

Easy Picnic Beans

1 small onion, chopped
2 teaspoons vegetable oil
2 cans (16 ounces each)
   HEINZ® Vegetarian
   Beans
¼ cup HEINZ® Tomato
   Ketchup
1 tablespoon brown sugar
   (optional)
1 teaspoon HEINZ®
   Worcestershire Sauce

Sauté onion in vegetable oil until tender. Stir in beans and remaining ingredients. Simmer, uncovered, 10 to 15 minutes or until desired consistency, stirring occasionally.

Makes 4 servings (about 3½ cups beans)

helpful hint:

To chop an onion, remove the skin and cut the onion in half through the root end with a utility knife. Place the onion half, cut side down, on a cutting board. Cut it into slices perpendicular to the root end, holding the onion with your fingers to keep it together. Turn the onion half and cut it crosswise. Repeat with the remaining half.

Fruity Wild Rice Side Dish

In skillet, melt margarine. Add walnuts and dried fruit; cook over low heat 5 minutes. Blend into wild rice. Sprinkle with brown sugar, if desired, and cinnamon.

Makes 6 servings

Favorite recipe from **Minnesota Cultivated Wild Rice Council**

¼ cup (½ stick) margarine
½ cup walnuts, coarsely chopped
½ cup diced dried fruit bits
3 cups cooked wild rice
Brown sugar (optional)
Ground cinnamon

Grilled Vegetables & Brown Rice

1. Cut zucchini lengthwise into thirds. Place all vegetables in large resealable plastic food storage bag; add dressing. Seal bag; refrigerate several hours or overnight.

2. Remove vegetables from marinade, reserving marinade. Place bell peppers and onion on grill over medium coals; brush with marinade. Grill 5 minutes. Turn vegetables over; add zucchini. Brush with marinade. Continue grilling until vegetables are crisp-tender, about 5 minutes, turning zucchini over after 3 minutes.

3. Remove vegetables from grill; coarsely chop. Add to hot rice; mix lightly. Season with salt and black pepper, if desired.

Makes 6 to 8 servings

Tip: Grilling adds a unique smokey flavor to vegetables and brings out their natural sweetness. The easiest way to grill vegetables is to cut them into large pieces and toss them in salad dressing or seasoned oil before grilling. Seasoned raw vegetables may also be wrapped tightly in foil packets and grilled until tender.

1 medium zucchini
1 medium red or yellow bell pepper, quartered lengthwise
1 small onion, cut crosswise into 1-inch-thick slices
¾ cup Italian dressing
4 cups hot cooked UNCLE BEN'S® Original Brown Rice

5
ingredients

Sweet Potatoes with Cranberry-Ginger Glaze

2 medium sweet potatoes
½ cup dried cranberries
¼ cup cranberry juice
¼ cup maple syrup
2 slices (⅛ inch thick) fresh ginger

1. Pierce potatoes all over with fork. Microwave on HIGH 10 minutes or until soft. Peel and cut potatoes into eighths; place in serving dish.

2. Meanwhile to prepare glaze, place cranberries, juice, syrup, ginger and dash black pepper in small saucepan. Cook over low heat 7 to 10 minutes or until syrupy. Discard ginger slices. Pour glaze over potatoes.   *Makes 4 servings*

Tri-Color Pasta
Prep Time: 5 minutes • **Cook Time:** 10 minutes

1 package (16 ounces) tri-color pasta, uncooked*
2 cups BIRDS EYE® frozen Green Peas
2 plum tomatoes, chopped *or* 1 red bell pepper, chopped
1 cup shredded mozzarella cheese
⅓ cup prepared pesto sauce (or to taste)

*Or, substitute 1 bag (16 ounces) frozen tortellini.

• In large saucepan, cook pasta according to package directions. Add peas during last 5 minutes of cooking; drain in colander. Rinse under cold water to cool.

• In large bowl, combine pasta, peas, tomatoes and cheese. Stir in pesto.   *Makes 4 servings*

BBQ Corn Wheels

Prep Time: 10 minutes • **Cook Time:** 10 minutes

4 ears corn on the cob, husked and cleaned
3 red, green or yellow bell peppers, cut into large chunks
¾ cup barbecue sauce
½ cup honey
¼ cup *French's®* Worcestershire Sauce
Vegetable cooking spray

1. Cut corn into 1-inch slices. Alternately thread corn and pepper chunks onto four metal skewers. (Pierce tip of skewer through center of corn wheel to thread.) Combine barbecue sauce, honey and Worcestershire.

2. Coat kabobs with vegetable cooking spray. Grill kabobs on greased rack over medium heat for 5 minutes. Cook 5 minutes more until corn is tender, turning and basting with barbecue sauce mixture. Serve any extra sauce on the side with grilled hamburgers, steaks or chicken. *Makes 4 servings*

Cheesy Rice Casserole

Prep Time: 15 minutes • **Cook Time:** 9 minutes

2 cups hot cooked rice
1⅓ cups *French's®* French Fried Onions, divided
1 cup sour cream
1 jar (16 ounces) medium salsa
1 cup (4 ounces) shredded Cheddar or taco blend cheese

MICROWAVE DIRECTIONS
1. Combine rice and ⅔ *cup* French Fried Onions in large bowl. Spoon half of the rice mixture into microwavable 2-quart shallow casserole. Spread sour cream over rice mixture.

2. Layer half of the salsa and half of the cheese over sour cream. Sprinkle with remaining rice mixture, salsa and cheese. Cover loosely with plastic wrap. Microwave on HIGH 8 minutes or until heated through. Sprinkle with remaining ⅔ *cup* onions. Microwave 1 minute or until onions are golden brown. *Makes 6 servings*

Four-Season Pasta Salad

8 ounces uncooked
    trumpet-shaped or
    spiral pasta
1½ cups cauliflower florets
1½ cups sliced carrots
1½ cups snow peas
½ cup prepared Italian or
    honey-mustard salad
    dressing

1. Cook pasta according to package directions, adding cauliflower, carrots and snow peas to saucepan during last 3 minutes of cooking time. Drain pasta and vegetables. Place under cold running water to stop cooking; drain again. Transfer to large bowl.

2. Add salad dressing to pasta and vegetable mixture; toss lightly to coat.

Makes 4 to 6 servings

Sautéed Zucchini and Yellow Squash

5 tablespoons unsalted
    butter
2 teaspoons Chef Paul
    Prudhomme's Vegetable
    Magic®
1 cup chopped onion
2 cups thinly sliced yellow
    squash*
2 cups thinly sliced
    zucchini*

*You can substitute cauliflower, carrots, broccoli or other vegetables of your choice for all or part of the squashes.

Melt the butter in a large skillet over high heat. Add the Vegetable Magic and stir until well blended. Add the onion and sauté until golden brown, about 5 minutes, stirring occasionally and scraping pan bottom well. Add the squashes and cook until somewhat tender but still crispy, about 2 minutes, stirring frequently and being sure that all of the vegetable slices are well coated with the butter. Serve immediately.

Makes 2 to 3 servings

Buffalo Chili Onions

Prep Time: 10 minutes • **Cook Time:** 10 minutes

½ cup *Frank's® RedHot®*
　Original Cayenne
　Pepper Sauce
½ cup (1 stick) butter or
　margarine, melted or
　olive oil
¼ cup Cattleman's® Award
　Winning Classic
　Barbecue Sauce
1 tablespoon chili powder
4 large sweet onions, cut
　into ½-inch-thick slices

1. Whisk together **Frank's RedHot** Sauce, butter, barbecue sauce and chili powder in medium bowl until blended; brush on onion slices.

2. Place onions on grid. Grill over medium-high coals 10 minutes or until tender, turning and basting often with the chili mixture. Serve warm.　　　　　　　　　　　　　　　*Makes 6 side-dish servings*

Tip: Onions may be prepared ahead and grilled just before serving.

Note: To make Grilled Buffalo Garlic Bread, combine ¼ cup each Frank's® Redhot® Sauce and melted butter with 1 teaspoon minced garlic. Lightly brush on thick slices of Italian bread. Grill or toast until golden. Top with blue cheese crumbles, if desired.

Asian Slaw

Prep Time: 5 minutes

½ cup HELLMANN'S® or
　BEST FOODS® Real
　Mayonnaise
2 tablespoons lime juice
2 tablespoons sugar
¾ teaspoon salt
¼ teaspoon ground ginger
1 bag (16 ounces) coleslaw
　mix
2 tablespoons chopped
　fresh cilantro (optional)

1. In large bowl, combine all ingredients except coleslaw mix and cilantro; stir until well blended.

2. Stir in coleslaw mix and cilantro. Chill, if desired.
　　　　　　　　　　　　　　　　　　　　Makes 4 servings

5 ingredients

Creamy Vegetables & Pasta

1 can (10¾ ounces)
   condensed cream of
   chicken soup,
   undiluted
1 cup milk
¼ cup grated Parmesan
   cheese
1 package (16 ounces)
   frozen seasoned pasta
   and vegetable
   combination
1⅓ cups *French's*® French
   Fried Onions, divided

MICROWAVE DIRECTIONS

1. Combine soup, milk and cheese in 2-quart microwavable shallow casserole. Stir in vegetable combination and ⅔ *cup* French Fried Onions. Microwave on HIGH 12 minutes* or until vegetables and pasta are crisp-tender, stirring halfway through cooking time.

2. Sprinkle with remaining ⅔ *cup* onions. Microwave 1 minute or until onions are golden. *Makes 6 servings*

Or, bake in preheated 350°F oven 30 to 35 minutes.

Tip: Add canned tuna or salmon for a great meatless dish. Serve with a salad on the side.

Sprightly Ruby Grapefruit Salad

4 cups torn leaf lettuce
1 tablespoon plus
   2 teaspoons finely
   chopped fresh mint *or*
   1 teaspoon dried mint
1 cup Texas Red Grapefruit
   sections, drained
¼ cup pecan halves, toasted
¼ cup prepared poppy seed
   dressing

Combine lettuce, mint, grapefruit and pecans in salad bowl; toss. Add dressing and toss well. *Makes 4 servings*

Favorite recipe from *TexaSweet Citrus Marketing, Inc.*

5 Hearty Main Dishes ingredients

Pantry Fruited Chicken

Prep Time: 5 to 10 minutes • **Cook Time:** 60 minutes

3 pounds chicken parts
1 bottle (12 ounces) LAWRY'S® Lemon Pepper Marinade, divided
1 can (29 ounces) yams or sweet potatoes, drained
1 cup canned apple pie filling
½ cup dried cranberries

Preheat oven to 375°F. Spray broiler pan bottom with nonstick cooking spray; arrange chicken skin-side-down on pan. Pour ⅔ cup Lemon Pepper Marinade over chicken. Bake for 30 minutes. Turn chicken over. Arrange yams, apple pie filling and cranberries around chicken. Pour remaining Marinade over fruit and chicken. Return pan to oven and bake 30 minutes or until chicken is thoroughly cooked. Spoon pan juices over chicken and fruit before serving. *Makes 4 to 6 servings*

Serving Suggestion: Serve with warm crusty bread or rice pilaf.

Variation: Try with LAWRY'S® Citrus Grill Marinade for another great flavor combination!

5
ingredients

15-Minute Chicken and Broccoli Risotto

1 small onion, chopped
2 pouches (about 9 ounces each) ready-to-serve yellow rice
2 cups frozen chopped broccoli
1 package (about 6 ounces) refrigerated fully cooked chicken breast strips, cut into pieces
½ cup chicken broth

1. Heat 1 tablespoon oil in large skillet over medium-high heat. Add onion; cook 3 minutes or until translucent.

2. Knead rice in bag. Add rice, broccoli, chicken and broth to onion in skillet. Cover; cook 6 to 8 minutes or until hot, stirring occasionally.

Makes 4 servings

Serving Suggestion: Top with toasted, sliced almonds for a crunchy texture and added flavor.

Quick Pork Fajitas

1 pork tenderloin, about 1 pound, thinly sliced
2 to 3 tablespoons fajita seasoning or marinade
½ onion, sliced
½ green bell pepper, sliced
4 to 6 flour tortillas, warmed

Toss pork pieces with fajita seasoning in shallow bowl. In large nonstick skillet over medium-high heat, stir-fry pork pieces with onion and green pepper until pork is cooked and vegetables are just tender. Wrap portions in flour tortillas; garnish with salsa.

Makes 4 servings

Favorite recipe from **National Pork Board**

helpful hint:

Raw meat is easier to slice thinly if it is partially frozen, so place the pork tenderloin in the freezer for about 20 minutes just prior to slicing it.

15–MINUTE CHICKEN AND BROCCOLI RISOTTO

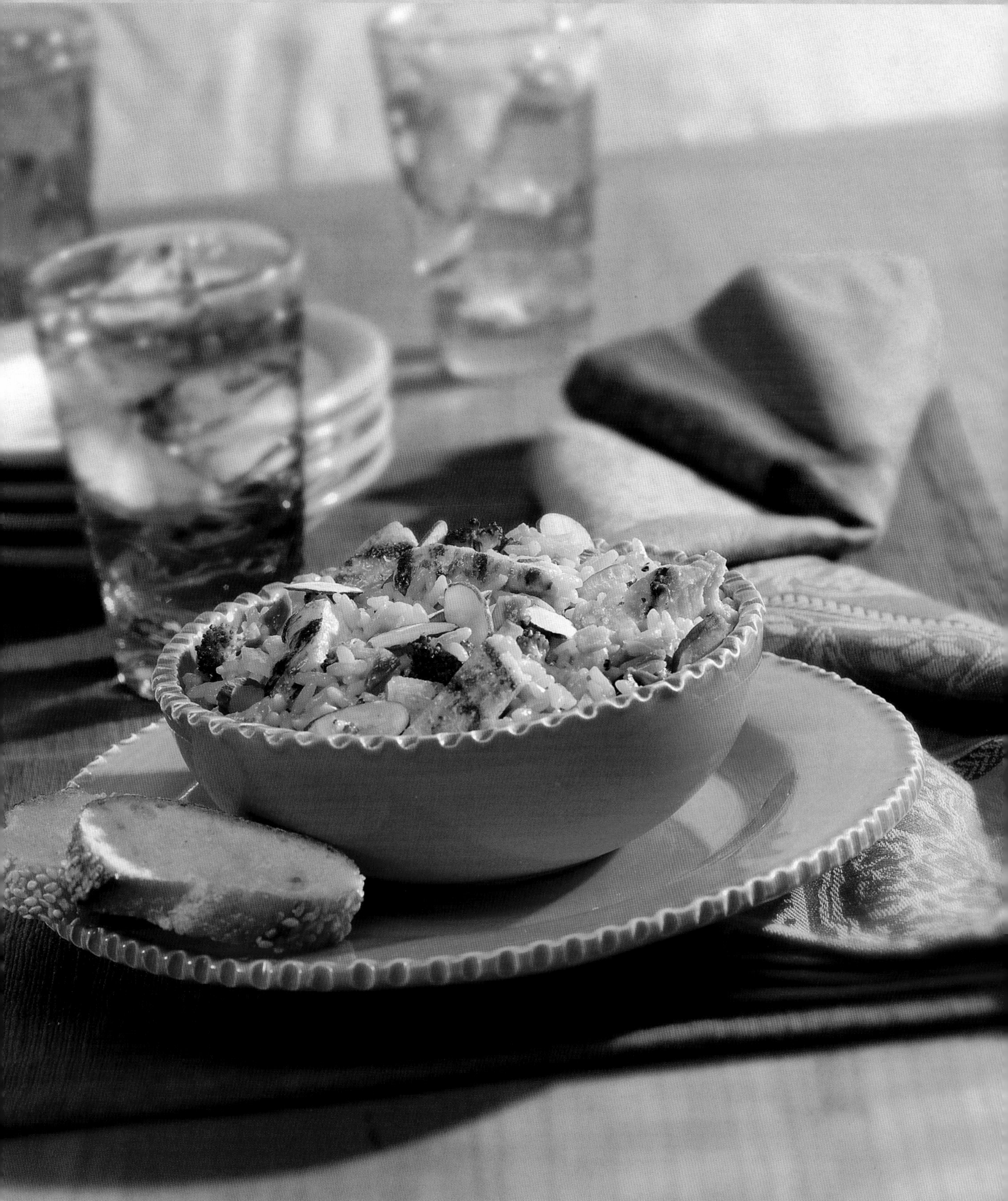

Spiced Turkey with Fruit Salsa

1 turkey breast tenderloin
 (about 6 ounces)
2 teaspoons lime juice
1 teaspoon mesquite
 seasoning blend or
 ground cumin
½ cup frozen pitted sweet
 cherries, thawed and
 cut into halves*
¼ cup chunky salsa

*Drained canned sweet cherries
can be substituted for frozen.

1. Prepare grill for direct grilling. Brush both sides of turkey with lime juice. Sprinkle with mesquite seasoning.

2. Grill turkey over medium heat 15 to 20 minutes or until turkey is no longer pink in center and juices run clear, turning once.

3. Meanwhile, combine cherries and salsa in medium bowl; stir until well blended.

4. Thinly slice turkey. To serve, spoon salsa mixture over turkey.

Makes 2 servings

Idaho Potato & Tuna Stove-Top Casserole

2½ pounds Idaho Potatoes,
 scrubbed and cut into
 bite-sized cubes (about
 7 cups)
1 (10-ounce) package
 frozen peas and carrots
1 (12-ounce) can tuna
 packed in water,
 drained
1 (10¾-ounce) can
 condensed Cheddar
 cheese soup, undiluted
¼ teaspoon garlic powder
¼ teaspoon black pepper

1. Bring 1½ quarts of water to a boil in medium saucepan. Add potatoes. Return to a boil and cook 5 minutes.

2. Add frozen vegetables. Return to a boil and cook 2 minutes (or to desired tenderness). Drain.

3. Stir tuna, soup and seasonings into same saucepan. Add hot potato mixture. Stir and serve. (Note: If necessary, reheat over very low heat. Add water if needed.)

Makes 6 servings

Serving Suggestion: Serve with green salad and vinaigrette dressing.

Favorite recipe from **Idaho Potato Commission**

SPICED TURKEY WITH FRUIT SALSA

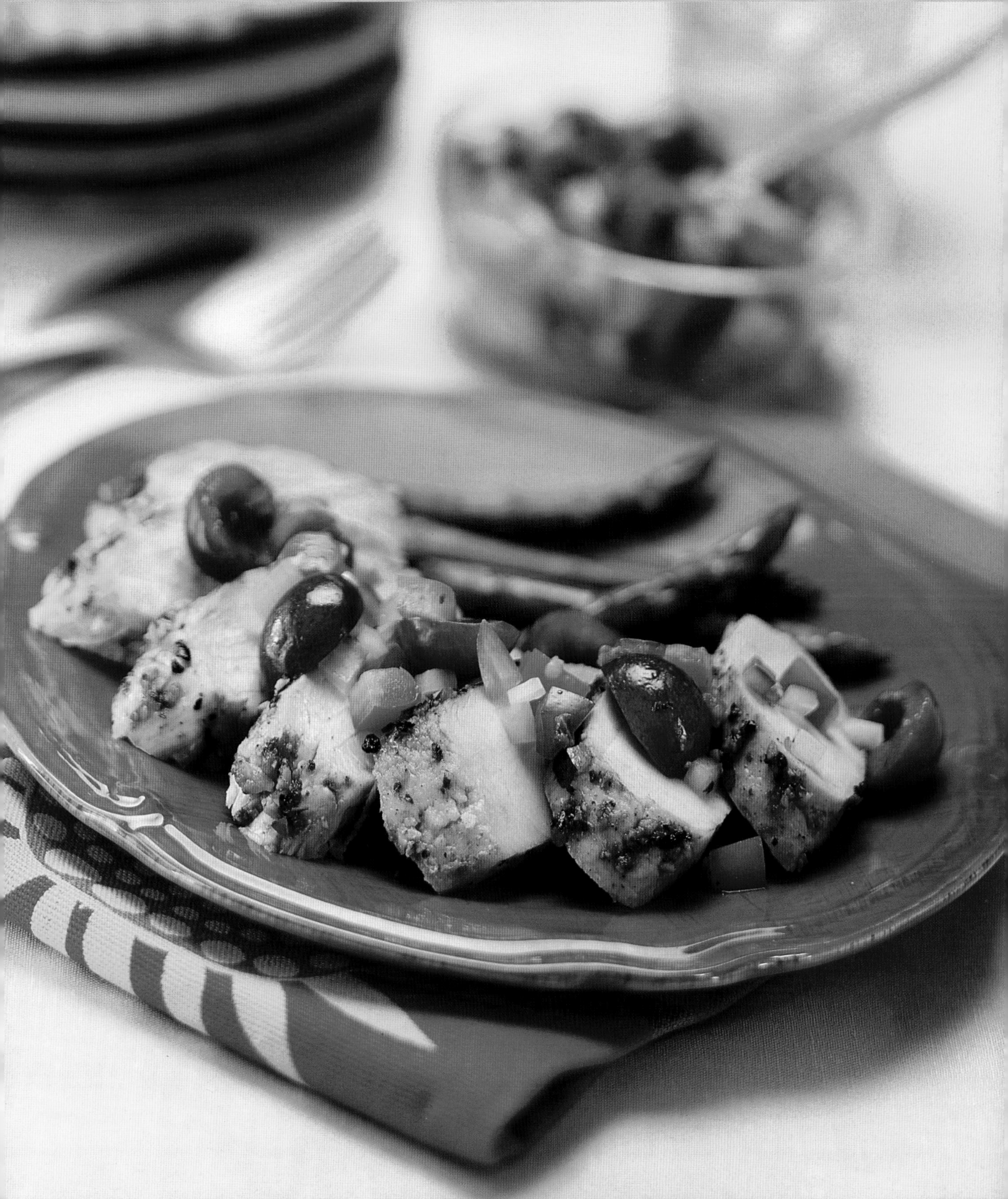

Groovy Angel Hair Goulash

Prep Time: 5 minutes • **Cook Time:** 15 minutes

1 pound lean ground beef
2 tablespoons margarine or butter
1 (4.8-ounce) package PASTA RONI® Angel Hair Pasta with Herbs
1 (14½-ounce) can diced tomatoes, undrained
1 cup frozen or canned corn, drained

1. In large skillet over medium-high heat, brown ground beef. Remove from skillet; drain. Set aside.

2. In same skillet, bring 1½ cups water and margarine to a boil.

3. Stir in pasta; cook 1 minute or just until pasta softens slightly. Stir in tomatoes, corn, beef and Special Seasonings; return to a boil. Reduce heat to medium. Gently boil uncovered, 4 to 5 minutes or until pasta is tender, stirring frequently. Let stand 3 to 5 minutes before serving. *Makes 4 servings*

Buttery Pepper and Citrus Broiled Fish

Prep Time: 5 minutes • **Cook Time:** 10 minutes

3 tablespoons MOLLY MCBUTTER® Flavored Sprinkles
1 tablespoon MRS. DASH® Lemon Pepper Blend
1 tablespoon lime juice
2 teaspoons honey
1 pound boneless white fish fillets

Combine first 4 ingredients in small bowl; mix well. Broil fish 6 to 8 inches from heat, turning once. Spread with Lemon Pepper mixture. Broil an additional 4 to 5 minutes. *Makes 4 servings*

helpful hint:

Fish cooks quickly. Be careful not to overcook it as this makes the fish tough and destroys the flavor. Fish is done when the flesh turns opaque and begins to flake easily when tested with a fork. Cooking times will vary with each fish and cut.

Rice and Chicken Wraps

8 boneless skinless chicken
    tenderloins
2 cups water
1 box UNCLE BEN'S® Fast
    Cook Recipe Long
    Grain & Wild Rice
½ cup ranch salad dressing
1 cup shredded lettuce
8 (10-inch) flour tortillas

1. Spray large skillet with nonstick cooking spray. Add chicken; cook over medium-high heat 10 to 12 minutes or until lightly browned on both sides. Add water, rice and contents of seasoning packet. Bring to a boil. Cover; reduce heat and simmer 10 minutes or until chicken is no longer pink in center and liquid is absorbed. Stir in salad dressing.

2. Spoon rice mixture evenly down center of each tortilla; top with lettuce. Fold in both sides of tortillas; roll up tortilla tightly from bottom, keeping filling firmly packed. Slice each wrap diagonally into 2 pieces.

Makes 4 servings

Texas Barbecued Ribs

1 cup GRANDMA'S®
    Molasses
½ cup coarse-grained
    mustard
2 tablespoons cider vinegar
2 teaspoons dry mustard
3½ pounds pork loin baby
    back ribs or spareribs,
    cut into 6 sections

Prepare grill for direct cooking. In medium bowl, combine molasses, coarse-grained mustard, cider vinegar and dry mustard. When ready to cook, place ribs on grill, meaty side up, over medium-hot coals. Grill 1 to 1 hour, 15 minutes or until meat is tender and starts to pull away from bone, basting frequently with sauce* during last 15 minutes of grilling. To serve, cut ribs apart carefully with knife and arrange on platter.

Makes 4 servings

Do not baste during last 5 minutes of grilling.

Italian Pork Chops

2 cups uncooked long-grain white rice
4 large pork chops (½ inch thick)
1 teaspoon basil, crushed
1 can (26 ounces) DEL MONTE® Spaghetti Sauce with Mushrooms or Chunky Italian Herb Spaghetti Sauce
1 green bell pepper, cut into thin strips

1. Cook rice according to package directions.

2. Preheat broiler. Sprinkle meat with basil; season with salt and black pepper, if desired. Place meat on broiler pan. Broil 4 inches from heat about 6 minutes on each side or until no longer pink in center.

3. Combine sauce and green pepper in microwavable dish. Cover with plastic wrap; slit to vent. Microwave on HIGH 5 to 6 minutes or until green pepper is tender-crisp and sauce is heated through. Add meat; cover with sauce. Microwave 1 minute. Serve over hot rice. *Makes 4 servings*

Serving Suggestion: Serve with baked potatoes and vegetables.

Turkey and Stuffing Pie

2 cups prepared stuffing
2 (5-ounce) cans HORMEL® chunk turkey, drained and flaked
1 cup shredded Swiss cheese
½ cup milk
3 eggs

Heat oven to 350°F. Pat stuffing evenly into 9-inch pie plate to form crust, building up side to form rim. Sprinkle turkey and cheese evenly over stuffing. In small bowl, beat together milk and eggs; pour over turkey. Bake 35 to 40 minutes or until knife inserted near center comes out clean. Let stand 5 minutes before serving. *Makes 6 servings*

5
ingredients

Garlic 'n Lemon Roast Chicken

1 small onion, finely
    chopped
1 envelope LIPTON®
    RECIPE SECRETS®
    Savory Herb with
    Garlic Soup Mix
2 tablespoons BERTOLLI®
    Olive Oil
2 tablespoons lemon juice
1 (3½-pound) roasting
    chicken

1. In large plastic bag or large bowl, combine onion and soup mix blended with oil and lemon juice; add chicken. Close bag and shake, or toss in bowl, until chicken is evenly coated. Cover and marinate in refrigerator, turning occasionally, 2 hours.

2. Preheat oven to 350°F. Place chicken and marinade in 13×9-inch baking or roasting pan. Arrange chicken, breast side up; discard bag.

3. Bake uncovered, basting occasionally, 1 hour 20 minutes or until meat thermometer reaches 180°F. (Insert meat thermometer into thickest part of thigh between breast and thigh; make sure tip does not touch bone.)
Makes 4 servings

Southwestern Enchiladas

1 can (10 ounces)
    enchilada sauce
2 packages (about 6 ounces
    each) refrigerated fully
    cooked steak strips*
4 (8-inch) flour tortillas
½ cup condensed nacho
    cheese soup, undiluted
    or ½ cup chile-flavored
    pasteurized process
    cheese spread
1½ cups (6 ounces) shredded
    Mexican cheese blend

*Fully cooked steak strips can be found in the refrigerated prepared meats section of the supermarket.

1. Preheat oven to 350°F. Spread half of enchilada sauce in 9-inch glass baking dish; set aside.

2. Place about 3 ounces steak down center of each tortilla. Top with 2 tablespoons cheese soup. Roll up tortillas; place seam side down in baking dish. Pour remaining enchilada sauce evenly over tortillas. Sprinkle with cheese. Bake 20 to 25 minutes or until heated through.
Makes 4 servings

Cutlets Milanese

Prep Time: 6 to 8 minutes • **Cook Time:** 6 minutes

1 package (about 1 pound)
  PERDUE® FIT 'N EASY®
  Thin-Sliced Turkey
  Breast Cutlets or
  Chicken Breast
  Salt and black pepper to
  taste
½ cup Italian seasoned
  bread crumbs
½ cup grated Parmesan
  cheese
1 large egg beaten with
  1 teaspoon water
2 to 3 tablespoons olive oil

Season cutlets with salt and pepper. On wax paper, combine bread crumbs and Parmesan cheese. Dip cutlets in egg mixture and roll in bread crumb mixture. In large nonstick skillet over medium-high heat, heat oil. Add cutlets and sauté 3 minutes per side until golden brown and cooked through. *Makes 4 servings*

Broccoli Chicken au Gratin

Prep Time: 5 minutes • **Cook Time:** 30 minutes

1 (6.5-ounce) package
  RICE-A-RONI® Broccoli
  Au Gratin
2½ tablespoons margarine or
  butter
¾ pound boneless, skinless
  chicken breasts, cut
  into thin strips
2 cups frozen chopped
  broccoli
1 cup fresh sliced
  mushrooms
¼ teaspoon coarse ground
  black pepper

1. In large skillet over medium heat, sauté rice-pasta mix with margarine until pasta is light golden brown.

2. Slowly stir in 2¼ cups water, chicken and Special Seasonings; bring to a boil. Reduce heat to low. Cover; simmer 10 minutes.

3. Stir in broccoli, mushrooms and pepper. Cover; cook 5 to 10 minutes or until rice is tender and chicken is no longer pink inside. Let stand 3 to 5 minutes before serving. *Makes 4 servings*

5

ingredients

Louisiana Stir-Fry

Prep Time: 15 minutes • **Cook Time:** 12 to 15 minutes

• In wok or large skillet, heat oil over medium-high heat.

• Add shrimp; stir-fry 2 to 3 minutes or until shrimp turn pink and opaque. Remove to serving plate.

• Add vegetables, green bell pepper and water to wok; cover and cook 4 to 6 minutes.

• Uncover; stir in tomatoes. Cook 3 to 4 minutes or until heated through and slightly thickened.

• Return shrimp to wok; cook and stir about 1 minute or until heated through. *Makes 4 servings*

Variation: Substitute 1 package (16 ounces) frozen fully cooked shrimp or 1 pound imitation crab legs. Add to cooked vegetables and cook until heated through.

2 tablespoons vegetable oil
1 pound raw medium
  shrimp, shelled and
  deveined *or* ½ pound
  sea scallops
1 bag (16 ounces) BIRDS
  EYE® frozen Broccoli,
  Corn & Red Peppers
½ green bell pepper,
  chopped
2 teaspoons water
1 can (14½ ounces) stewed
  tomatoes, drained

Garden Ranch Linguine with Chicken

8 ounces linguine, cooked and drained
2 cups cooked mixed vegetables, such as broccoli, cauliflower and bell peppers
2 cups cubed cooked chicken
1 cup HIDDEN VALLEY® The Original Ranch® Salad Dressing
1 tablespoon grated Parmesan cheese

Combine all ingredients except cheese in a large saucepan; toss well. Heat through; sprinkle with cheese before serving.

Makes 4 servings

Bistro Steak with Mushrooms

Prep Time: 10 minutes • **Cook Time:** 20 minutes

1½ to 2 pounds boneless sirloin steak (1½ inches thick)
2 cups sliced mushrooms
1 can (10¾ ounces) condensed golden mushroom soup, undiluted
½ cup dry red wine or beef broth
3 tablespoons *French's®* Worcestershire Sauce

1. Rub both sides of steak with *¼ teaspoon pepper*. Heat *1 tablespoon oil* over medium-high heat in nonstick skillet. Cook steak about 5 minutes per side for medium-rare or to desired doneness. Transfer steak to platter.

2. Stir-fry mushrooms in same skillet in *1 tablespoon oil* until browned. Stir in soup, wine, Worcestershire and *¼ cup water*. Bring to a boil. Simmer, stirring, 3 minutes. Return steak and juices to skillet. Cook until heated through. Serve with mashed potatoes, if desired.

Makes 6 servings

5
ingredients

Hearty BBQ Beef Sandwiches

1 envelope LIPTON®
    RECIPE SECRETS®
    Onion Soup Mix
2 cups water
½ cup chili sauce
¼ cup firmly packed light
    brown sugar
1 (3-pound) boneless chuck
    roast
8 kaiser rolls or hamburger
    buns, toasted

1. Preheat oven to 325°F. In Dutch oven or 5-quart heavy ovenproof saucepan, combine soup mix, water, chili sauce and sugar; add roast.

2. Cover and bake 3 hours or until roast is tender.

3. Remove roast; reserve juices. Bring reserved juices to a boil over high heat. Boil 4 minutes.

4. Meanwhile, with fork, shred roast. Stir roast into reserved juices and simmer, stirring frequently, 1 minute. Serve on rolls.

Makes 8 servings

helpful hint:

Always measure brown sugar in a dry measure cup and pack down firmly. To soften hardened brown sugar, place in glass dish with 1 slice of bread. Cover with plastic wrap and microwave at HIGH 30 to 40 seconds. Let stand 30 seconds; stir. Remove bread.

5 Tantalizing Treats ingredients

Rocky Road Candy

Prep Time: 10 minutes • **Chill Time:** 2 hours

2 cups (12 ounces)
   semisweet chocolate
   chips
2 tablespoons butter or
   margarine
1 (14-ounce) can EAGLE
   BRAND® Sweetened
   Condensed Milk
   (NOT evaporated milk)
2 cups dry roasted peanuts
1 (10½-ounce) package
   miniature
   marshmallows

1. In heavy saucepan, over low heat, melt chocolate chips and butter with EAGLE BRAND®; remove from heat.

2. In large bowl, combine peanuts and marshmallows; stir in chocolate mixture. Spread in wax paper lined 13×9-inch baking pan. Chill 2 hours or until firm.

3. Remove candy from pan; peel off paper and cut into squares. Store loosely covered at room temperature.

Makes about 3½ dozen candies

Microwave Directions: In 1-quart glass measure, combine chocolate chips, butter and EAGLE BRAND®. Microwave at HIGH (100% power) 3 minutes, stirring after 1½ minutes. Stir until chocolate chips are melted and smooth. Let stand 5 minutes. Proceed as directed above.

Refreshing Cocoa-Fruit Sherbet

1 ripe medium banana
1½ cups orange juice
1 cup (½ pint) half-and-half
½ cup sugar
¼ cup HERSHEY'S Cocoa

1. Slice banana into blender container. Add orange juice; cover and blend until smooth. Add remaining ingredients; cover and blend well. Pour into 8- or 9-inch square pan. Cover; freeze until hard around edges.

2. Spoon partially frozen mixture into blender container. Cover; blend until smooth but not melted. Pour into 1-quart mold. Cover; freeze until firm. Unmold onto cold plate and slice. Garnish as desired. *Makes 8 servings*

Variation: Add 2 teaspoons orange-flavored liqueur with orange juice.

Peachy Chocolate Yogurt Shake

⅔ cup peeled fresh peach slices *or* 1 package (10 ounces) frozen peach slices, thawed and drained
¼ teaspoon almond extract
2 cups (1 pint) vanilla nonfat frozen yogurt
¼ cup HERSHEY'S Syrup
¼ cup nonfat milk

1. Place peaches and almond extract in blender container. Cover; blend until smooth.

2. Add frozen yogurt, syrup and milk. Cover; blend until smooth. Serve immediately. *Makes 4 servings*

5

ingredients

Pink Peppermint Meringues

3 egg whites
⅛ teaspoon peppermint
    extract
5 drops red food coloring
½ cup superfine sugar*
6 peppermint candies,
    finely crushed

*Or substitute ½ cup
granulated sugar processed
in food processor 1 minute
until very fine.*

1. Preheat oven to 200°F. Line 2 cookie sheets with parchment paper; set aside.

2. Beat egg whites in medium bowl with electric mixer at medium-high speed about 45 seconds or until frothy. Stir in peppermint extract and food coloring. Add sugar, 1 tablespoon at a time, while mixer is running. Continue beating until egg whites are stiff and glossy.

3. Drop meringue by teaspoonfuls into 1-inch mounds on prepared cookie sheets; sprinkle evenly with crushed peppermint candies.

4. Bake 2 hours or until meringues are dry when tapped. Transfer parchment paper with meringues to wire racks to cool completely. When cool, peel meringues off parchment; store in airtight container.

Makes about 6 dozen meringues

helpful hint:

Eggs separate more easily when cold. To separate an egg yolk from a white, gently tap the egg in the center with a table knife or against a hard surface, such as the side of a bowl. Gently break the egg in half over a small bowl. Holding a shell half in each hand, gently transfer the yolk back and forth between the two shell halves, allowing the white to drip into the bowl. Place the yolk into another bowl. An egg separator is a useful tool that will make this job even easier.

Pecan Sables

1 package (18 ounces)
   refrigerated sugar
   cookie dough
½ cup sugar
¼ teaspoon ground
   cinnamon
2 cups finely chopped
   pecans
1½ cups pecan halves

1. Preheat oven to 350°F. Lightly grease cookie sheets. Let dough stand at room temperature about 15 minutes.

2. Combine sugar and cinnamon in small bowl; set aside. Combine dough and chopped pecans in large bowl; beat until well blended.

3. Shape dough into 1-inch balls; roll in cinnamon-sugar. Place balls 2 inches apart on prepared cookie sheets. Press 1 pecan half into each dough ball.

4. Bake 8 to 10 minutes or until edges are light brown. Cool 2 minutes on cookie sheets. Remove to wire racks; cool completely.   *Makes about 3 dozen cookies*

Strawberry Chantilly
Prep Time: 20 minutes

1 box (10 ounces) BIRDS
   EYE® frozen
   Strawberries
1 cup heavy cream*
2 tablespoons sugar*
½ teaspoon vanilla extract*
   Belgian waffles or pound
   cake slices, toasted

*For extra-quick preparation,
substitute 2 cups thawed frozen
whipped topping for cream,
sugar and vanilla.*

• Thaw strawberries according to package directions until partially thawed. Mash strawberries in bowl.

• Beat cream, sugar and vanilla in large bowl until stiff peaks form. Gently fold in ¼ cup mashed strawberries.

• Spoon remaining strawberries over waffles. Top with whipped cream mixture.   *Makes about 4 servings*

White Chocolate Pudding Parfaits

1 package (4-serving size) instant white chocolate pudding mix
2 cups milk
¾ cup whipping cream
1½ cups fresh raspberries or sliced strawberries
2 tablespoons chopped pistachio nuts

1. Add pudding mix to milk in medium bowl; beat with wire whisk or electric mixer 2 minutes. Refrigerate 5 minutes or until thickened. Beat whipping cream in small deep bowl with electric mixer at high speed until stiff peaks form. Fold whipped cream into pudding.

2. In each of 4 parfait or wine glasses, layer ¼ cup pudding and 2 tablespoons raspberries; repeat layers. Spoon remaining pudding over berries. Serve immediately or cover and chill up to 6 hours before serving. Sprinkle with nuts just before serving.

Makes 4 servings

Fluffy Orange Pie

Prep Time: 10 minutes • **Chill Time:** 2 hours

1 (8-ounce) package cream cheese, softened
1 (14-ounce) can sweetened condensed milk
1 (6-ounce) can frozen orange juice concentrate, thawed
1 cup whipping cream, whipped
1 (6-ounce) READY CRUST® Graham Cracker Pie Crust

1. Beat cream cheese in large bowl with electric mixer until fluffy; gradually beat in sweetened condensed milk, then orange juice concentrate, until smooth. Fold in whipped cream.

2. Pour into crust.

3. Chill 2 hours or until set. Garnish as desired. Refrigerate leftovers.

Makes 8 servings

5
ingredients

Tropical Breeze Smoothies

1 cup frozen pineapple
   chunks
1 cup frozen mango chunks
½ cup unsweetened
   coconut milk
½ cup milk
2 tablespoons honey

1. Place all ingredients in blender. Cover; process 15 to 30 seconds or until smooth, using on/off pulsing action to break up chunks.

2. Divide smoothie between 2 glasses; serve immediately.

Makes 2 (1-cup) servings

Vanilla Flan

¾ cup granulated sugar
1 can (12 fluid ounces)
   NESTLÉ® CARNATION®
   Evaporated Milk
1 can (14 ounces) NESTLÉ®
   CARNATION®
   Sweetened Condensed
   Milk
3 large eggs
1 tablespoon vanilla extract

PREHEAT oven to 325°F.

HEAT sugar in small, *heavy-duty* saucepan over medium-low heat, stirring constantly, for 3 to 4 minutes or until dissolved and caramel colored. Quickly pour onto bottom of deep-dish 9-inch pie plate; swirl around bottom and side to coat.

COMBINE evaporated milk, sweetened condensed milk, eggs and vanilla extract in medium bowl. Pour into prepared pie plate. Place pie plate in large roasting pan; fill roasting pan with warm water to about 1-inch depth.

BAKE for 45 to 50 minutes or until knife inserted near center comes out clean. Remove flan from water. Cool on wire rack. Refrigerate for 4 hours or overnight.

TO SERVE: Run small spatula around edge of pie plate. Invert serving plate over pie plate. Turn over; shake gently to release. Caramelized sugar forms sauce.

Makes 8 servings

No-Bake Chocolate Peanut Butter Bars

2 cups peanut butter, *divided*
¾ cup (1½ sticks) butter, softened
2 cups powdered sugar
3 cups graham cracker crumbs
2 cups (12-ounce package) NESTLÉ® TOLL HOUSE® Semi-Sweet Chocolate Mini Morsels, *divided*

GREASE 13×9-inch baking pan.

BEAT *1¼* cups peanut butter and butter in large mixer bowl until creamy. Gradually beat in *1 cup* powdered sugar. With hands or wooden spoon, work in *remaining* powdered sugar, graham cracker crumbs and *½ cup* morsels. Press evenly into prepared pan. Smooth top with spatula.

MELT *remaining* peanut butter and *remaining* morsels in medium, *heavy-duty* saucepan over *lowest possible heat*, stirring constantly, until smooth. Spread over graham cracker crust in pan. Refrigerate for at least 1 hour or until chocolate is firm; cut into bars. Store in refrigerator. *Makes 5 dozen bars*

Cornflake Pudding

4 cups cornflakes
1 egg
4 cups milk
⅔ cup GRANDMA'S® Molasses
1 teaspoon salt
1 teaspoon ground cinnamon

Heat oven to 300°F. Place cornflakes in 1½-quart soufflé dish. Beat egg in large bowl; add milk, molasses, salt and cinnamon. Pour over cornflakes; mix well. Bake for 1 hour, 30 minutes.

Makes 4 servings

Poached Pears in Cranberry Syrup

Prep Time: 40 minutes

1 quart (4 cups) cranberry juice
1 cup KARO® Light Corn Syrup
8 slices (¼ inch thick) unpeeled fresh ginger
2 cinnamon sticks (2 to 3 inches)
8 slightly underripe pears

1. In heavy 4-quart saucepot combine cranberry juice, corn syrup, ginger and cinnamon sticks; bring to a boil over medium-high heat.

2. Peel pears, leaving stems attached. Add to cranberry liquid; cover. Reduce heat and simmer 15 to 20 minutes or until pears are tender. With slotted spoon transfer pears to shallow serving dish.

3. Remove ginger slices and cinnamon sticks. Discard all but 2 cups syrup in saucepot. Bring to a boil; boil 10 to 12 minutes or until syrup thickens slightly. Spoon sauce over pears.

Makes 8 servings

Mississippi Mud Brownies

1 (21-ounce) package DUNCAN HINES® Family-Style Chewy Fudge Brownie Mix
2 eggs
⅓ cup water
⅓ cup vegetable oil plus additional for greasing
1 jar (7 ounces) marshmallow creme
1 container DUNCAN HINES® Milk Chocolate Frosting, melted

1. Preheat oven to 350°F. Grease bottom only of 13×9-inch baking pan.

2. Combine brownie mix, eggs, water and oil in large bowl. Stir with spoon until well blended, about 50 strokes. Spread in pan. Bake at 350°F for 25 to 28 minutes or until set.

3. Spread marshmallow creme gently over hot brownies. Pour 1¼ cups melted milk chocolate frosting over marshmallow creme. Swirl with knife to marble. Cool completely. Cut into bars.

Makes 20 to 24 brownies

Note: Store leftover melted frosting in original container in refrigerator.

Chocolate Mint Truffles

1¾ cups (11.5-ounce package) NESTLÉ® TOLL HOUSE® Milk Chocolate Morsels
1 cup (6 ounces) NESTLÉ® TOLL HOUSE® Semi-Sweet Chocolate Morsels
¾ cup heavy whipping cream
1 tablespoon peppermint extract
1½ cups finely chopped walnuts, toasted, or NESTLÉ® TOLL HOUSE® Baking Cocoa

LINE baking sheet with wax paper.

PLACE milk chocolate and semi-sweet morsels in large mixer bowl. Heat cream to a gentle boil in small saucepan; pour over morsels. Let stand for 1 minute; stir until smooth. Stir in peppermint extract. Cover with plastic wrap; refrigerate for 35 to 45 minutes or until slightly thickened. Stir just until color lightens slightly. (*Do not* overmix or truffles will be grainy.)

DROP by rounded teaspoon onto prepared baking sheet; refrigerate for 10 to 15 minutes. Shape into balls; roll in walnuts or cocoa. Store in airtight container in refrigerator.

Makes about 48 truffles

Variation: After rolling chocolate mixture into balls, freeze for 30 to 40 minutes. Microwave 1¾ cups (11.5-ounce package) NESTLÉ® TOLL HOUSE® Milk Chocolate Morsels and 3 tablespoons vegetable shortening in medium, uncovered, microwave-safe bowl on MEDIUM-HIGH (70%) power for 1 minute. STIR. Morsels may retain some of their original shape. If necessary, microwave at additional 10- to 15-second intervals, stirring just until morsels are melted. Dip truffles into chocolate mixture; shake off excess. Place on foil-lined baking sheets. Refrigerate for 15 to 20 minutes or until set. Store in airtight container in refrigerator.

5
ingredients

Rich Chocolate Mousse

1 cup (6 ounces) NESTLÉ®
    TOLL HOUSE® Semi-
    Sweet Chocolate
    Morsels
3 tablespoons butter, cut
    into pieces
2 teaspoons TASTER'S
    CHOICE® 100% Pure
    Instant Coffee
1 tablespoon hot water
2 teaspoons vanilla extract
½ cup heavy whipping
    cream

MICROWAVE morsels and butter in medium, uncovered, microwave-safe bowl on HIGH (100%) power for 1 minute. STIR. Morsels may retain some of their original shape. If necessary, microwave at additional 10- to 15-second intervals, stirring just until morsels are melted. Dissolve Taster's Choice in hot water; stir into chocolate. Stir in vanilla extract; cool to room temperature.

WHIP cream in small mixer bowl on high speed until stiff peaks form; fold into chocolate mixture. Spoon into tall glasses; refrigerate for 1 hour or until set. Garnish as desired.

Makes 2 servings

Blueberry and Citrus Sorbet "Layer Cake"

½ cup finely chopped
    walnuts
¼ cup plus 2 tablespoons
    blueberry preserves or
    jam, divided
1 pint orange sorbet,
    slightly softened
1 pint lemon or other citrus
    sorbet, slightly softened
1 cup fresh blueberries

Line the bottom and sides of an 8×4-inch loaf pan with a double layer of waxed paper, folding the paper to fit smoothly. In a small bowl, stir together walnuts and ¼ cup of the blueberry preserves; set aside. Spoon orange sorbet into the lined pan, smoothing the top to make an even layer. Spread the reserved walnut-preserves mixture evenly over the orange sorbet. Spoon the lemon sorbet evenly over the preserves and smooth the top. Cover tightly with aluminum foil. Freeze several hours or overnight. Just before serving, in a medium bowl, stir remaining 2 tablespoons preserves until smooth; fold in fresh blueberries. Invert the cake onto a chilled serving plate. Remove the pan and waxed paper; spoon about one-fourth of the blueberry mixture down the center of the cake. Cut the cake into 8 (1-inch) slices. Serve on chilled dessert plates; top each slice with a spoonful of the remaining fresh berry mixture. Serve immediately. *Makes 8 servings*

Favorite recipe from **US Highbush Blueberry Council**

5 ingredients

Turtle Caramel Apples

4 large Golden Delicious or
   Granny Smith apples
4 craft sticks*
1 package (14 ounces)
   caramels
2 tablespoons water
2 jars (3½ ounces each)
   macadamia nuts or
   pecans, coarsely
   chopped
1 bittersweet or semisweet
   chocolate candy bar
   (about 2 ounces),
   broken into small
   pieces

*Available where cake
decorating supplies are sold.*

1. Line 13X9-inch baking pan with waxed paper; set aside. To prepare apples, wash and dry completely. Remove stems. Insert craft sticks into centers of apples.

2. Combine caramels and water in small saucepan. Simmer over low heat until caramels melt and mixture is smooth, stirring frequently.

3. Immediately dip apples, one at a time, into caramel to cover completely. Scrape excess caramel from bottom of apple onto side of saucepan, letting excess drip back into saucepan.

4. Immediately roll apples in nuts to lightly coat, pressing nuts lightly with fingers so they stick to caramel. Place apples, stick-side up, on prepared baking sheet. Let stand 20 minutes or until caramel is set.

5. Place chocolate in small resealable food storage bag; seal bag. Microwave on MEDIUM (50%) 1 minute. Turn bag over; microwave on MEDIUM 1 minute more or until melted. Knead bag until chocolate is smooth. Cut off tiny corner of bag; pipe or drizzle chocolate decoratively onto apples.

6. Let apples stand 30 minutes or until chocolate is set. Store loosely covered in refrigerator up to 3 days. Let stand at room temperature 15 minutes before serving.   *Makes 4 apples*

my favorites...............................

My Favorite Recipes

Favorite recipe: _____

Favorite recipe from: _____

Ingredients: _____

_____

_____

_____

_____

_____

Method: _____

_____

_____

_____

_____

_____

_____

_____

_____

_____

_____

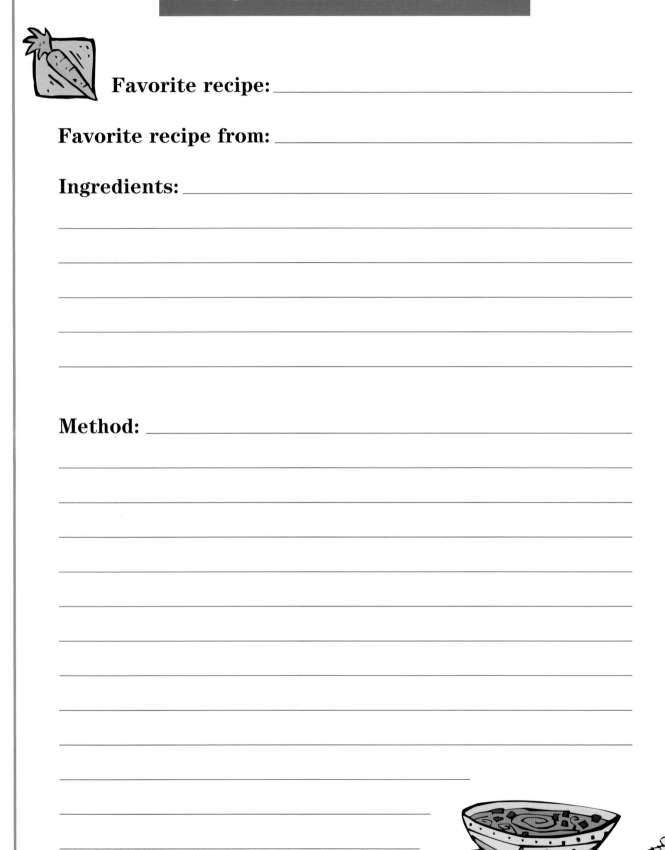

Favorite recipe: _____

Favorite recipe from: _____

Ingredients: _____

_____

_____

_____

_____

_____

Method: _____

_____

_____

_____

_____

_____

_____

_____

_____

_____

_____

_____

_____

My Favorite Recipes

Favorite recipe: _____

Favorite recipe from: _____

Ingredients: _____

_____

_____

_____

_____

_____

Method: _____

_____

_____

_____

_____

_____

_____

_____

_____

_____

_____

_____

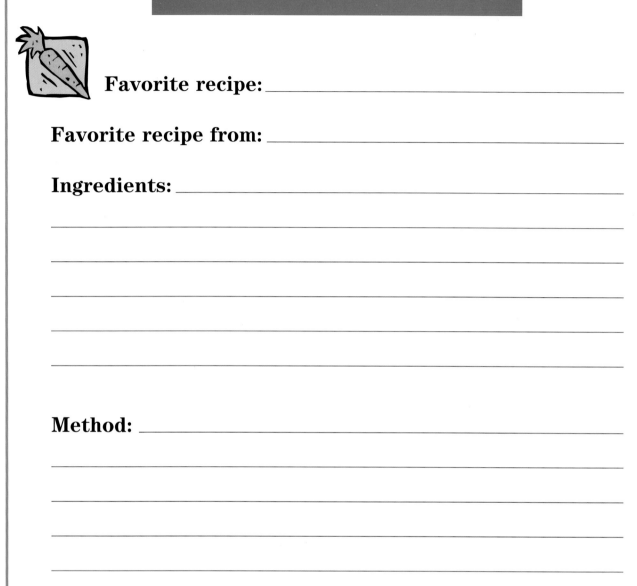

Favorite recipe: _____

Favorite recipe from: _____

Ingredients: _____

_____

_____

_____

_____

_____

Method: _____

_____

_____

_____

_____

_____

_____

_____

_____

_____

_____

_____

_____

244

My Favorite Recipes

Favorite recipe: _____

Favorite recipe from: _____

Ingredients: _____

_____

_____

_____

_____

_____

Method: _____

_____

_____

_____

_____

_____

_____

_____

_____

_____

_____

_____

My Favorite Recipes

Favorite recipe: _____

Favorite recipe from: _____

Ingredients: _____

_____

_____

_____

_____

_____

Method: _____

_____

_____

_____

_____

_____

_____

_____

_____

_____

_____

_____

Favorite recipe: _____

Favorite recipe from: _____

Ingredients: _____

_____

_____

_____

_____

_____

Method: _____

_____

_____

_____

_____

_____

_____

_____

_____

_____

_____

_____

My Favorite Recipes

Favorite recipe: _____

Favorite recipe from: _____

Ingredients: _____

_____

_____

_____

_____

_____

_____

Method: _____

_____

_____

_____

_____

_____

_____

_____

_____

_____

_____

_____

Favorite recipe: _____

Favorite recipe from: _____

Ingredients: _____

_____

_____

_____

_____

_____

Method: _____

_____

_____

_____

_____

_____

_____

_____

_____

_____

_____

_____

My Favorite Recipes

Favorite recipe: _____

Favorite recipe from: _____

Ingredients: _____

_____

_____

_____

_____

_____

_____

Method: _____

_____

_____

_____

_____

_____

_____

_____

_____

_____

_____

_____

Favorite recipe: _____

Favorite recipe from: _____

Ingredients: _____

_____

_____

_____

_____

_____

Method: _____

_____

_____

_____

_____

_____

_____

_____

_____

_____

_____

_____

_____

My Favorite Recipes

Favorite recipe: _____

Favorite recipe from: _____

Ingredients: _____

_____

_____

_____

_____

_____

Method: _____

_____

_____

_____

_____

_____

_____

_____

_____

_____

_____

Favorite recipe: _____

Favorite recipe from: _____

Ingredients: _____

_____

_____

_____

_____

_____

Method: _____

_____

_____

_____

_____

_____

_____

_____

_____

_____

_____

_____

My Favorite Recipes

Favorite recipe: _____

Favorite recipe from: _____

Ingredients: _____

_____

_____

_____

_____

_____

Method: _____

_____

_____

_____

_____

_____

_____

_____

_____

_____

_____

_____

Favorite recipe: _____

Favorite recipe from: _____

Ingredients: _____

_____

_____

_____

_____

_____

Method: _____

_____

_____

_____

_____

_____

_____

_____

_____

_____

_____

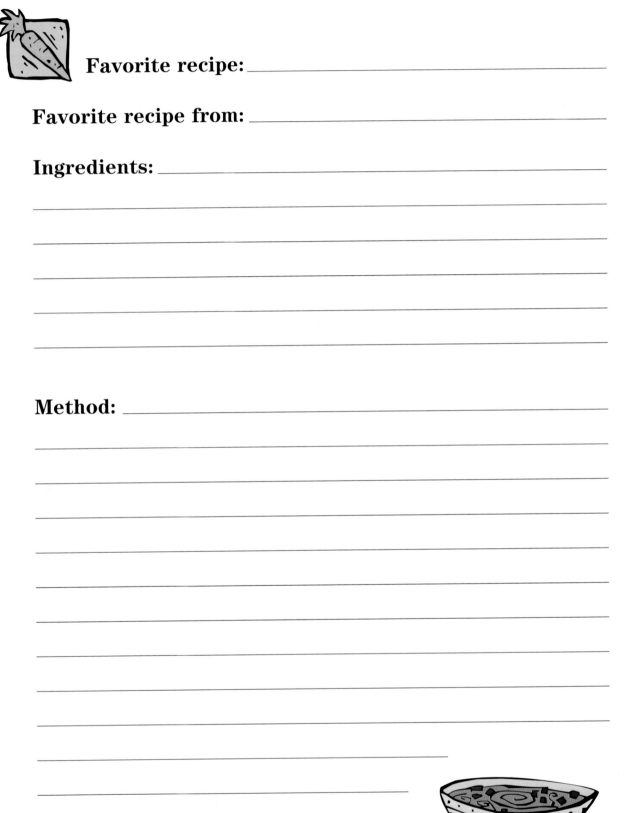

My Favorite Recipes

Favorite recipe: _____

Favorite recipe from: _____

Ingredients: _____

_____

_____

_____

_____

_____

Method: _____

_____

_____

_____

_____

_____

_____

_____

_____

_____

_____

Favorite recipe: _____

Favorite recipe from: _____

Ingredients: _____

_____

_____

_____

_____

_____

Method: _____

_____

_____

_____

_____

_____

_____

_____

_____

_____

_____

_____

My Favorite Recipes

Favorite recipe: _____

Favorite recipe from: _____

Ingredients: _____

_____

_____

_____

_____

_____

Method: _____

_____

_____

_____

_____

_____

_____

_____

_____

_____

_____

Favorite recipe: _____

Favorite recipe from: _____

Ingredients: _____

_____

_____

_____

_____

_____

Method: _____

_____

_____

_____

_____

_____

_____

_____

_____

_____

_____

_____

Favorite recipe: _____

Favorite recipe from: _____

Ingredients: _____

_____

_____

_____

_____

_____

Method: _____

_____

_____

_____

_____

_____

_____

_____

_____

_____

_____

_____

My Favorite Dinner Party

Date: _____

Occasion: _____

_____

Guests: _____

_____

_____

_____

_____

Menu: _____

_____

_____

_____

_____

_____

_____

_____

_____

_____

My Favorite Dinner Party

Date: _____

Occasion: _____
_____

Guests: _____
_____
_____
_____
_____

Menu: _____
_____
_____
_____
_____
_____
_____
_____
_____
_____
_____

My Favorite Dinner Party

Date: _____

Occasion: _____

_____

Guests: _____

_____

_____

_____

_____

Menu: _____

_____

_____

_____

_____

_____

_____

_____

_____

_____

_____

My Favorite Dinner Party

Date: _____

Occasion: _____

_____

Guests: _____

_____

_____

_____

_____

Menu: _____

_____

_____

_____

_____

_____

_____

_____

_____

_____

_____

My Favorite Dinner Party

Date: _____

Occasion: _____

_____

Guests: _____

_____

_____

_____

_____

Menu: _____

_____

_____

_____

_____

_____

_____

_____

_____

_____

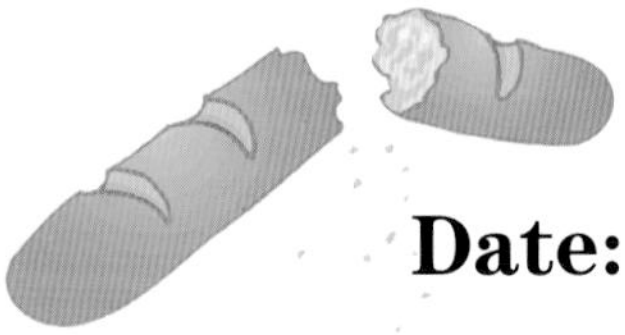

Date: _____

Occasion: _____

_____

Guests: _____

_____

_____

_____

_____

Menu: _____

_____

_____

_____

_____

_____

_____

_____

_____

_____

_____

_____

_____

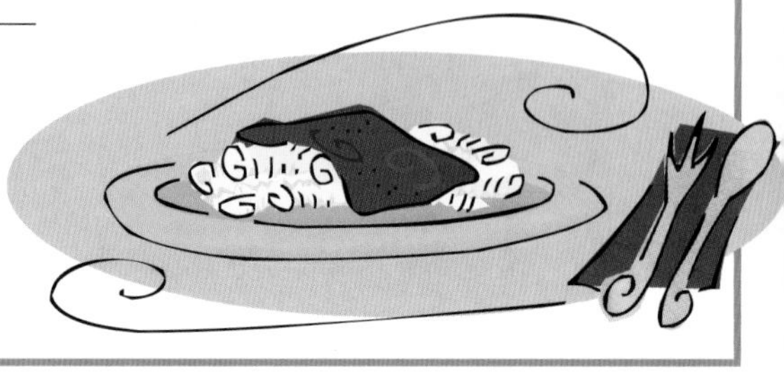

_____

My Favorite Potluck

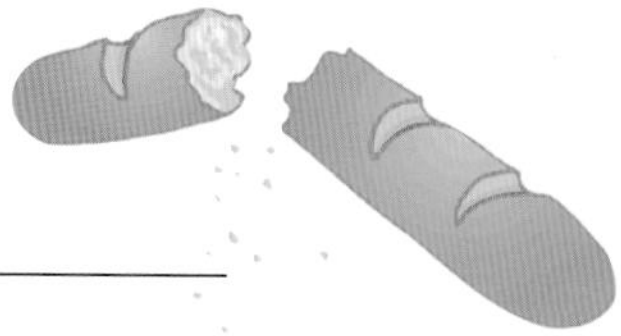

Date: _____

Occasion: _____

_____

Guests: _____

_____

_____

_____

_____

Menu: _____

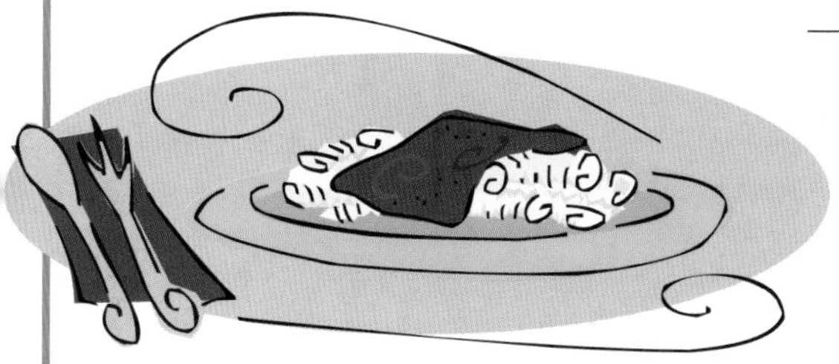

_____

_____

_____

_____

_____

_____

_____

_____

_____

_____

_____

My Favorite Potluck

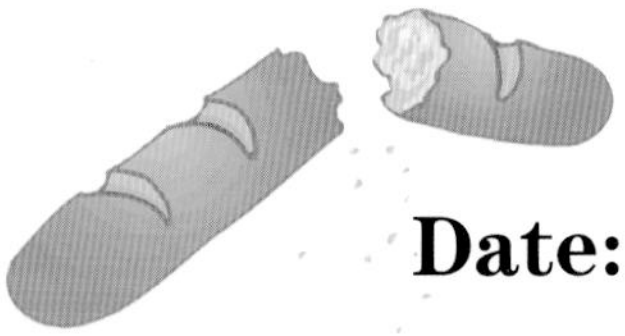

Date: _____

Occasion: _____

_____

Guests: _____

_____

_____

_____

Menu: _____

_____

_____

_____

_____

_____

_____

_____

_____

_____

_____

_____

_____

My Favorite Food Gifts

Friend: _____

Date: _____

Food Gift: _____

_____

_____

_____

_____

_____

_____

_____

_____

_____

_____

_____

_____

_____

_____

_____

_____

Friend: _____

Date: _____

Food Gift: _____

_____

_____

_____

_____

_____

_____

_____

_____

_____

_____

_____

_____

_____

_____

_____

_____

_____

270

My Favorite Friends

Friend: _____

Favorite foods: _____

_____

_____

_____

_____

_____

Don't serve: _____

_____

_____

_____

_____

_____

_____

_____

_____

_____

_____

_____

_____

271

Friend: _____

Favorite foods: _____

_____

_____

_____

_____

_____

Don't serve: _____

_____

_____

_____

_____

_____

_____

_____

_____

_____

_____

_____

_____

hints, tips & index

Casserole Cookware

Casserole cookware comes in a variety of shapes, sizes and materials that fall into 2 general descriptions. They can be either deep, round containers with handles and tight-fitting lids or square and rectangular baking dishes. Casseroles are made out of glass, ceramic or metal. When making a casserole, it's important to bake the casserole in the proper size dish so that the ingredients cook evenly in the time specified.

Size Unknown?

If the size of the casserole or baking dish isn't marked on the bottom of the dish, it can be measured to determine the size.

• Round and oval casseroles are measured by volume, not inches, and are always listed by quart capacity. Fill a measuring cup with water and pour it into an empty casserole. Repeat until the casserole is filled with water, keeping track of the amount of water added. The amount of water is equivalent to the size of the dish.

• Square and rectangular baking dishes are usually measured in inches. If the dimensions aren't marked on the bottom of a square or rectangular baking dish, use a ruler to measure on top from the inside of one edge to the inside of the edge across.

Helpful Preparation Techniques

Some of the recipes call for advance preparations, such as cooked chicken or pasta. In order to ensure success when following and preparing the recipes, here are several preparation tips and techniques.

• Tips for Cooking Pasta

For every pound of pasta, bring 4 to 6 quarts of water to a full, rolling boil. Gradually add pasta, allowing water to return to a boil. Stir frequently to prevent the pasta from sticking together.

Pasta is finished cooking when it is tender but still firm to the bite, or al dente. The pasta continues to cook when the casserole is placed in the oven so it is

273

important that the pasta be slightly undercooked. Otherwise, the more the pasta cooks, the softer it becomes and, eventually, it will fall apart.

Immediately drain pasta to prevent overcooking. For best results, combine pasta with other ingredients immediately after draining.

• Tips for Cooking Rice
The different types of rice require different amounts of water and cooking times. Follow the package instructions for the best results.

Measure the amount of water specified on the package and pour into a medium saucepan. Bring to a boil over medium-high heat. Slowly add rice and return to a boil. Reduce heat to low. Cover and simmer for the time specified on the package or until the rice is tender and most of the water has been absorbed.

To test the rice for doneness, bite into a grain or squeeze a grain between your thumb and index finger. The rice is done when it is tender and the center is not hard.

• Tips for Chopping and Storing Fresh Herbs
To chop fresh herbs, place in glass measuring cup. Snip herbs into small pieces with kitchen scissors.

Wrap remaining fresh herbs in a slightly damp paper towel and place in an airtight food storage bag. Store up to 5 days in the refrigerator.

Top it Off!
Buttery, golden brown bread crumbs are a popular choice when it comes to topping a casserole but the selections shouldn't end there. Be creative with the many choices available to jazz up an old favorite or just vary how they are used. Crispy toppings can be crushed, partially crushed, broken into bite-size pieces or left whole. Fruits, vegetables and other toppings

can be chopped, sliced or shredded. Sprinkle a new spice or herb in place of another one. All the toppings can be placed on top of the casserole in a variety of ways–a small amount in the center, around the edges as a border or in straight or diagonal lines across the top.

Crispy toppings add a nice texture to your casseroles. Choose from crushed unsweetened cereals; potato, corn, tortilla or bagel chips; pretzels; flour or corn tortilla strips; plain or flavored croutons; flavored crackers; crumbled bacon; ramen or chow mein noodles; sesame seeds; French fried onions and various nuts. As a guide, add 1 tablespoon melted margarine to ½ cup crushed crumbs. Sprinkle over casserole and bake to add buttery flavor.

Fruits, vegetables and other toppings add a burst of color to most casseroles. Add green, red or white onions; orange or lemon peel; mushrooms; dried or fresh fruits, such as apples, apricots, cranberries, dates, oranges, pineapple and raisins; olives; bell or chili peppers; bean sprouts; tomatoes; avocados; celery; corn; coconut; carrots; fresh herbs and shredded cheeses according to what flavor and look you desire. In order to keep the fruits and vegetables bright and crisp, add them 5 minutes before the casserole is finished cooking or sprinkle them on after it's out of the oven.

• Homemade Bread Crumbs

Making your own bread crumbs is a great way to use up the rest of a fresh loaf. To make bread crumbs, preheat oven to 300°F. Place a single layer of bread slices on a baking sheet and bake 5 to 8 minutes or until completely dry and lightly browned. Cool completely. Process in food processor or crumble in resealable plastic food storage bag until very fine. For additional flavor, season with salt, pepper and a small amount of dried herbs, ground spices or grated cheese as desired. Generally, 1 slice of bread equals ⅓ cup bread crumbs.

The Basics

• As with conventional cooking recipes, slow cooker recipe time ranges are provided to account for variables such as temperature of ingredients before cooking, how full the slow cooker is and even altitude. Once you become familiar with your slow cooker you'll have a good idea which end of the time range to use.

• Manufacturers recommend that slow cookers should be one-half to three-quarters full for best results.

• Keep a lid on it! The slow cooker can take as long as twenty minutes to regain the heat lost when the cover is removed. If the recipe calls for stirring or checking the dish near the end of the cooking time, replace the lid as quickly as you can.

• To clean your slow cooker, follow the manufacturer's instructions. To make cleanup even easier, spray with nonstick cooking spray before adding food.

• Always taste the finished dish before serving and adjust seasonings to your preference. Consider adding a dash of any of the following: salt, pepper, seasoned salt, seasoned herb blends, lemon juice, soy sauce, Worcestershire sauce, flavored vinegar, freshly ground pepper or minced fresh herbs.

TIPS & TECHNIQUES

Adapting Recipes

If you'd like to adapt your own favorite recipe to a slow cooker, you'll need to follow a few guidelines. First, try to find a similar recipe in this publication or your manufacturer's guide. Note the cooking times, liquid, quantity and size of meat and vegetable pieces. Because the slow cooker captures moisture, you will want to reduce the amount of liquid, often by as much as half. Add dairy products toward the end of the cooking time so they do not curdle.

Selecting the Right Meat

A good tip to keep in mind while shopping is that you can, and in fact should, use tougher, inexpensive cuts of meat. Top-quality cuts, such as loin chops or filet mignon, fall apart during long cooking periods. Keep those for roasting, broiling or grilling and save money when you use your slow cooker. You will be amazed to find even the toughest cuts come out fork-tender and flavorful.

Cutting Your Vegetables

Vegetables often take longer to cook than meats. Cut vegetables into small, thin pieces and place them on the bottom or near the sides of the slow cooker. Pay careful attention to the recipe instructions in order to cut vegetables to the proper size.

Foil to the Rescue

To easily lift a dish or a meat loaf out of the slow cooker, make foil handles according to the following directions.

• Tear off three 18×3-inch strips of heavy-duty foil. Crisscross the strips so they resemble the spokes of a wheel. Place your dish or food in the center of the strips.

• Pull the foil strips up and place into the slow cooker. Leave them in while you cook so you can easily lift the item out when ready.

Food Safety Tips

If you do any advance preparation, such as trimming meat or cutting vegetables, make sure you keep the food covered and refrigerated until you're ready to start cooking. Store uncooked meats and vegetables separately. If you are preparing meat, poultry or fish, remember to wash your cutting board, utensils and hands before touching other foods.

Once your dish is cooked, don't keep it in the slow cooker too long. Foods need to be kept cooler than 40°F or hotter than 140°F to avoid the growth of harmful bacteria. Remove food to a clean container and cover and refrigerate as soon as possible. Do not reheat leftovers in the slow cooker. Use a microwave oven, the range-top or the oven for reheating.

Baking Tips

• Read the entire recipe before you begin to be sure you have all the necessary ingredients and utensils.

• Remove butter, margarine and cream cheese from the refrigerator to soften, if necessary.

•Adjust oven racks and preheat the oven. Check oven temperature with an oven thermometer to make sure the temperature is accurate.

• Toast and chop nuts and melt butter and chocolate before preparing batter or dough.

• Always use the pan size suggested in the recipe. Prepare pans as directed.

• Choose cookie sheets that fit in your oven with at least 1 inch on all sides between the edge of the sheet and the oven wall.

• Grease cookie sheets only when the recipe recommends it; otherwise, the cookies may spread too much.

• Measure the ingredients accurately and assemble them in the order they are listed in the recipe.

• When baking more than one sheet of cookies at a time, it's best to rotate them for even baking. Halfway through the baking time, rotate the cookie sheets from front to back as well as from the top rack to the bottom rack.

• Always check for doneness at the minimum baking time given in the recipe.

How Much of This=That

How much of this equals that?

Beans	1 cup = 6½ ounces 1 pound = 2½ cups 1 (8-ounce) package = 2¼ cups
Cheese	1 cup shredded = 4 ounces ¼ pound = 1 cup grated
Chicken	1 large boned breast = 2 cups cubed cooked meat
Garlic	2 medium cloves = 1 teaspoon minced
Herbs	1 tablespoon fresh = 1 teaspoon dried
Lemons	1 medium = 1 to 3 tablespoons juice and 2 to 3 teaspoons grated peel
Mushrooms	1 pound = about 6 cups sliced
Onions, yellow	1 medium = ½ to ¾ cup chopped 1 pound = about 6 cups sliced
Peppers, bell	1 large = 1 cup chopped
Rice, brown, uncooked	1 cup = 3 to 4 cups cooked
Rice, long grain uncooked	1 cup = 3 cups cooked 1 pound = 2¼ cups, uncooked
Shrimp	1 pound = 10 to 15 jumbo 1 pound = 16 to 20 large 1 pound = 25 to 30 medium
Tomatoes	1 pound (3 medium) = 1½ cups peeled and seeded

If I Don't Have This?

If you don't have:	Use:
1 cup beef or chicken broth	1 bouillon cube or 1 teaspoon granules mixed with 1 cup boiling water
1 small clove garlic	⅛ teaspoon garlic powder
1 tablespoon prepared mustard	1 teaspoon dry mustard
1 cup tomato sauce	½ cup tomato paste plus ½ cup cold water
1 teaspoon vinegar	2 teaspoons lemon juice
1 tablespoon cornstarch	2 tablespoons all-purpose flour or 2 teaspoons arrowroot
1 cup whole milk	1 cup skim milk plus 2 tablespoons melted butter
1 cup sweetened whipped cream	4½ ounces thawed frozen whipped topping
1 cup heavy cream (for baking, not whipping)	¾ cup whole milk plus ½ cup water
1 cup honey	1¼ cups granulated sugar plus ¼ cup water
1 whole egg	2 egg yolks plus 1 teaspoon cold water
1 cup sour cream	1 cup plain yogurt
½ cup firmly packed brown sugar	½ cup sugar mixed with 2 tablespoons molasses
3 ounces (3 squares) semisweet baking chocolate	3 ounces (½ cup) semisweet chocolate morsels

Is It Done Yet?

Use the following guides to test for doneness.

CASSEROLES
until hot and bubbly
until heated through
until cheese melts

MEAT

Beef
medium   140°F to 145°F
well done 160°F

Veal
medium   145°F to 150°F
well done 160°F

Lamb
medium   145°F
well done 160°F

Pork
well done 165°F to 170°F

POULTRY

Chicken
until temperature in thigh
  is 180°F (whole bird)
until chicken is no longer
  pink in center
until temperature in breast
  is 170°F

SEAFOOD

Fish
until fish begins to flake
  against the grain when
  tested with fork

Shrimp
until shrimp are pink and
  opaque

SAUCES
until (slightly) thickened

SOUPS
until heated through

STEWS
until meat is tender
until vegetables are tender

VEGETABLES
until crisp-tender
until tender
until browned

Metric Conversion Chart

VOLUME MEASUREMENTS (dry)

⅛ teaspoon = 0.5 mL
¼ teaspoon = 1 mL
½ teaspoon = 2 mL
¾ teaspoon = 4 mL
1 teaspoon = 5 mL
1 tablespoon = 15 mL
2 tablespoons = 30 mL
¼ cup = 60 mL
⅓ cup = 75 mL
½ cup = 125 mL
⅔ cup = 150 mL
¾ cup = 175 mL
1 cup = 250 mL
2 cups = 1 pint = 500 mL
3 cups = 750 mL
4 cups = 1 quart = 1 L

VOLUME MEASUREMENTS (fluid)

1 fluid ounce (2 tablespoons) = 30 mL
4 fluid ounces (½ cup) = 125 mL
8 fluid ounces (1 cup) = 250 mL
12 fluid ounces (1½ cups) = 375 mL
16 fluid ounces (2 cups) = 500 mL

WEIGHTS (mass)

½ ounce = 15 g
1 ounce = 30 g
3 ounces = 90 g
4 ounces = 120 g
8 ounces = 225 g
10 ounces = 285 g
12 ounces = 360 g
16 ounces = 1 pound = 450 g

DIMENSIONS

1/16 inch = 2 mm
⅛ inch = 3 mm
¼ inch = 6 mm
½ inch = 1.5 cm
¾ inch = 2 cm
1 inch = 2.5 cm

OVEN TEMPERATURES

250°F = 120°C
275°F = 140°C
300°F = 150°C
325°F = 160°C
350°F = 180°C
375°F = 190°C
400°F = 200°C
425°F = 220°C
450°F = 230°C

BAKING PAN SIZES

Utensil	Size in Inches/Quarts	Metric Volume	Size in Centimeters
Baking or Cake Pan (square or rectangular)	8×8×2	2 L	20×20×5
	9×9×2	2.5 L	23×23×5
	12×8×2	3 L	30×20×5
	13×9×2	3.5 L	33×23×5
Loaf Pan	8×4×3	1.5 L	20×10×7
	9×5×3	2 L	23×13×7
Round Layer Cake Pan	8×1½	1.2 L	20×4
	9×1½	1.5 L	23×4
Pie Plate	8×1¼	750 mL	20×3
	9×1¼	1 L	23×3
Baking Dish or Casserole	1 quart	1 L	—
	1½ quart	1.5 L	—
	2 quart	2 L	—

Acknowledgments

The publisher would like to thank the companies and organizations listed below for the use of their recipes and photographs in this publication.

ACH Food Companies, Inc.
Alouette® Cheese, Chavrie® Cheese, Saladena®
BelGioioso Cheese, Inc.
Birds Eye Foods
Bob Evans®
Cabot® Creamery Cooperative
Chef Paul Prudhomme's Magic Seasoning Blends®
Cherry Marketing Institute
Del Monte Corporation
Dole Food Company, Inc.
Duncan Hines® and Moist Deluxe® are registered trademarks of Pinnacle Foods Corp.
EAGLE BRAND®
Filippo Berio® Olive Oil
Florida Department of Agriculture and Consumer Services, Bureau of Seafood and Aquaculture
The Golden Grain Company®
Grandma's® is a registered trademark of Mott's, LLP
Heinz North America
The Hershey Company
The Hidden Valley® Food Products Company
Hillshire Farm®
Holland House® is a registered trademark of Mott's, LLP
Hormel Foods, LLC
Hostess®
Idaho Potato Commission

Jennie-O Turkey Store®
JOLLY TIME® Pop Corn
Keebler® Company
MASTERFOODS USA
Mauna La'i® is a registered trademark of Mott's, LLP
McIlhenny Company (TABASCO® brand Pepper Sauce)
Minnesota Cultivated Wild Rice Council
Mrs. Dash®
National Chicken Council / US Poultry & Egg Association
National Honey Board
National Pork Board
National Watermelon Promotion Board
Nestlé USA
Newman's Own, Inc.®
North Dakota Wheat Commission
Ortega®, A Division of B&G Foods, Inc.
Pacific Northwest Canned Pear Service
Perdue Farms Incorporated
Reckitt Benckiser Inc.
Southeast United Dairy Industry Association, Inc.
The Sugar Association, Inc.
TexaSweet Citrus Marketing, Inc.
U.S. Highbush Blueberry Council
Unilever
Veg•All®
Washington Apple Commission
Washington State Fruit Commission
Wisconsin Milk Marketing Board

283

Index

Index

Index